Yanmar

YANMAR MARINE DIESEL ENGINE D27A & D36A

Service Manual

Yanmar

YANMAR MARINE DIESEL ENGINE D27A & D36A

Service Manual

ISBN/EAN: 9783954272976
Erscheinungsjahr: 2013
Erscheinungsort: Bremen, Deutschland

© maritimepress in Europäischer Hochschulverlag GmbH & Co. KG, Fahrenheitstr. 1, 28359 Bremen. Alle Rechte beim Verlag und bei den jeweiligen Lizenzgebern.

www.maritimepress.de | office@maritimepress.de

Bei diesem Titel handelt es sich um den Nachdruck eines historischen, lange vergriffenen Buches. Da elektronische Druckvorlagen für diese Titel nicht existieren, musste auf alte Vorlagen zurückgegriffen werden. Hieraus zwangsläufig resultierende Qualitätsverluste bitten wir zu entschuldigen.

YANMAR
SERVICE MANUAL

ISO 9001 *Certified*

DIESEL OUTBOARD MOTOR

FOREWORD

This service manual outlines procedures for servicing and maintaining YANMAR D27A/D36A DIESEL OUTBOARD MOTOR to obtain maximum life and performance.
It explains about the structure, performance, disassembly and reassembly procedures, important inspection points, servicing instructions and the wear limit of parts. For full understanding of this manual, also refer to the Operation Manual and Parts Catalog. Besides reference use at your service shop, this manual can also be used as a text for your service engineers.
A full understanding of the content of this manual leads to accurate and efficient services. Good servicing guarantees the machine's performance and prevents troubles.
Please note that there may be changes in the structure explanations or maintenance instructions resulting from future improvements in quality and performance. If you have any questions, please contact us.

For accurate and efficient work, the following preparations are necessary:
1. Check the customer's service chart
    1) When was the last service?
    2) How many months or hours has the machine been used since the last service?
    3) What was the trouble and what parts were replaced in the last service?
    4) What parts must be replaced in the present service?
2. Preparation of parts
    Check the inventory of parts that are necessary for servicing.
3. Preparation of report forms
    Inspection and service check sheets, parts measurement record forms and operation test record forms.
4. Prepare the servicing tools, measuring instruments and containers, etc.

MODEL D27A & D36A

CHAPTER 1 GENERAL
1. Specifications 1-1
2. Exterior View 1-3
3. Cross-sectional View 1-10

CHAPTER 2 DISASSEMBLY AND REASSEMBLY
1. Preparations Before Disassembly and Reassembly 2-1
2. Tools, Measuring Instruments and Service Equipment 2-2
3. Exploded View of Parts 2-12
4. Reassembly Procedures 2-14
5. Reassembly Procedures for Drive Unit 2-29

CHAPTER 3 INSPECTION AND SERVICE PROCEDURES FOR ENGINE PARTS
1. Inspection and Service Procedures for Engine Parts 3-1
2. Cylinder Block 3-2
3. Piston and Connecting Rod 3-4
4. Crankshaft 3-7
5. Camshaft 3-8
6. Cylinder Head 3-9
7. Valve Arm Case 3-13
8. Intake/Exhaust Valve Arm and Unit Injector 3-14
9. Thermostat 3-17
10. Unit Injector 3-18
11. Governor 3-24

CHAPTER 4 REASSEMBLING AND SERVICING OF DRIVE UNIT
1. Swivel/Steering Bracket 4-1
2. Clamp Bracket 4-4
3. Upper Case 4-5
4. Bottom Cowling and Fitting Parts 4-6
5. Lower Gear Case 4-9
6. Cooling Water Pump and Cooling Water Piping 4-15
7. Steering Handle 4-16
8. Hydraulic Cylinder 4-17
9. Electric-Hydraulic Tilting 4-18
10. Connecting the Upper Case with Steering Bracket 4-20

CHAPTER 5 PIPING DIAGRAM
1. Piping Diagram 5-1

CHAPTER 6 ELECTRIC EQUIPMENT
1. Generator 6-1
2. Starting Motor (Reduction Gear) 6-2
3. Warning Device 6-4
4. Wiring Diagram 6-6

CHAPTER 7 SERVICE STANDARD
1. Service Standard Table (Engine) 7-1
2. Service Standard Table (Drive Unit) 7-3

CHAPTER 8 MAIN BOLT TIGHTENING TORQUE
1. Main Bolt Tightening Torque 8-1

CHAPTER 9 BACKLASH ADJUSTMENT
1. Backlash Adjustment 9-1

CHAPTER 10 PERIODICAL INSPECTION
1. Periodical Inspection Table 10-1

CHAPTER 11 OPTION
1. Diesel Outboard Propeller Guard Holes 11-1

Printed in Japan
A0A5055-JC03

CHAPTER 1
GENERAL

1. Specifications 1-1
2. Exterior View 1-3
3. Cross-sectional View 1-10

Chapter 1 General
1. Specifications

1. Specifications

1-1 D27A and D36A series

	Model			D27A				D36A			
				XE	XEP	YE	Y	XE	XEP	YE	YEP
Main item	Overall length	(mm)		730		1128 (When folding the handle 730)		759		1157 (When folding the handle 759)	
	Overall width	(mm)		392		430		437		449	
	Overall height	(mm)	L	1380	←	1434	1417	1438	←	←	←
			LL	1443	←	1493	1480	1501	←	←	←
			UL	1505	←	1559	1542	1563	←	←	←
			SUL	1710	←	1639	1622	—	—	—	—
	Transom length	(mm)	L	560	←	←	←	←	←	←	←
			LL	623	←	←	←	←	←	←	←
			UL	685	←	←	←	←	←	←	←
			SUL	765	←	←	←	←	←	←	←
	*1) Weight	(kg)	L	94	102	95	92	116	120	116	120
			LL	95	103	96	93	117	121	117	121
			UL	96	104	97	94	118	122	118	122
			SUL	97	105	98	95	—	—	—	—
	Tilt system			Manual	Hydraulic	Manual	Manual	Manual	Hydraulic	Manual	Hydraulic
	Starting system			Electric	Electric	Electric	Recoil	Electric	Electric	Electric	Electric
	Steering system			Remote control	Remote control	Bar handle	Bar handle	Remote control	Remote control	Bar handle	Bar handle
	Max. Output			19.9KW (27HP) / 4500rpm				26.5KW (36HP) / 4500rpm			
Engine	Type			4 cycle water cooled, Vertical Crankshaft Diesel Engine							
	No. of cylinders			3							
	Bore × Stroke	(mm)		70 × 70				82 × 70			
	Displacement	(ℓ)		808				1109			
	Combustion system			Direct injection by M-type unit injector							
	Brake mean effective pressure			0.70MPa (7.18kgf/cm²)				0.68MPa (6.98kgf/cm²)			
	Mean piston speed			10.5m/s							
	Max. combustion pressure / compression ratio			≤ 9.8MPa (100kgf/cm²) /19.2							
	Piston head clearance / valve clearance			0.60±0.05mm/0.2mm				0.55±0.05mm/0.2mm			
	Fuel injection timing			FIC 12° b.T.D.C				FIC 15° b.T.D.C			
	Fuel injection nozzle			YDLLA-P-type hole nozzle 4− φ0.2mm				YDLLA-P-type hole nozzle 5− φ0.22mm			
	Fuel injection valve opening pressure			19.61±0.49 MPa(200±5 kgf/cm²)							
	Firing order			1 —240°— 2 —240°— 3 —240°— 1							
	Direction of revolution			Clockwise (viewed from flywheel side)							
	Power take-off direction			Counter-flywheel side							
	Driving system of intake / exhaust valve and fuel pump			O.H.C. system driven by timing belt							
	Intake system			Intake inertia flow pipe							
	Exhaust system			Cooling water mixing and underwater exhaust system							
	Lubricating system			Forced lubrication by trochoid pump							
	Lube oil sump capacity	Full amount		2.4 ℓ				3.0 ℓ			
		Effective amount		1.0 ℓ				1.3 ℓ			
	Type of lube oil			API service grade CD class SAE 15W−40							

Chapter 1 General
1. Specifications

	Model	D27A				D36A			
		XE	XEP	YE	Y	XE	XEP	YE	YEP
Engine	Cooling system	Direct seawater cooling by rubber impeller pump							
	Fuel feed system	Pressure-feeding by trochoid pump							
	Governor type	Mechanical floating lever type							
	Starter capacity	12V − 1.2KW			—	12V − 1.4KW			
	Generator type / capacity	Dynamo house in flywheel / 12V − 10A							
	Battery capacity	12V−100A			—	12V − 100AH or more			
Fuel equipment	Fuel tank type/capacity	Portable / 24 ℓ							
	Fuel pipe	Returned to tank when overflowing, with primary valve, with one-touch joint on the fuel tank side							
Steering equipment	Steering angle	Max. 40 degrees right−to−left							
	Speed control system and angle	Remote control system	Bar handle grip revolving system 85°			Remote control system		Bar handle grip revolving system 85°	
	Tilting step and angle	4 steps 7°−23°	Power tilt (Arbitrary)	4 steps 7°−23°		5 steps 8°−24°	Power tilt (Arbitrary)	5 steps 8°−24°	Power tilt (Arbitrary)
	Max. tilting up angle	76°	76°	76°		76°	76°	76°	76°
	Angle when running in shallow sea	32° (〃)	Less than 2000 rpm	32° (When tilting angle is 7°)		32° (〃)	Less than 2000 rpm	32° (〃)	Less than 2000 rpm
	Hull mounting	Bolted to transom plate							
Driving equipment	Clutch type and operation	Dog type, clutch lever operation							
	Reduction gear type	Bevel gear							
	Reduction ratio (forward / reverse)	1.846 / 1.846							
	Lubrication system	Oil bath							
	Lube oil capacity	0.55 ℓ							
	Type of oil	Gear oil API service grade SAE 80W−90							
Propeller	Driving (damping) system	Spline and rubber press−fitting type							
	Direction of rotation	Clockwise (viewed from propeller side)							
	Max. rpm (forward / reverse)	2438 rpm / 1356−1625rpm							
	Number of blades−diameter × pitch	3−266.7 × 203 〜 3−266.7 × 330 (11 types)				3−292.1 × 228.6〜 3−292.1 × 381 (10 types)			

*1) Dry weight of outboard motor

Chapter 1 General
2. Exterior View   SM/D27A & D36A

2. Exterior View

2-1 D27A series

(1) D27AX

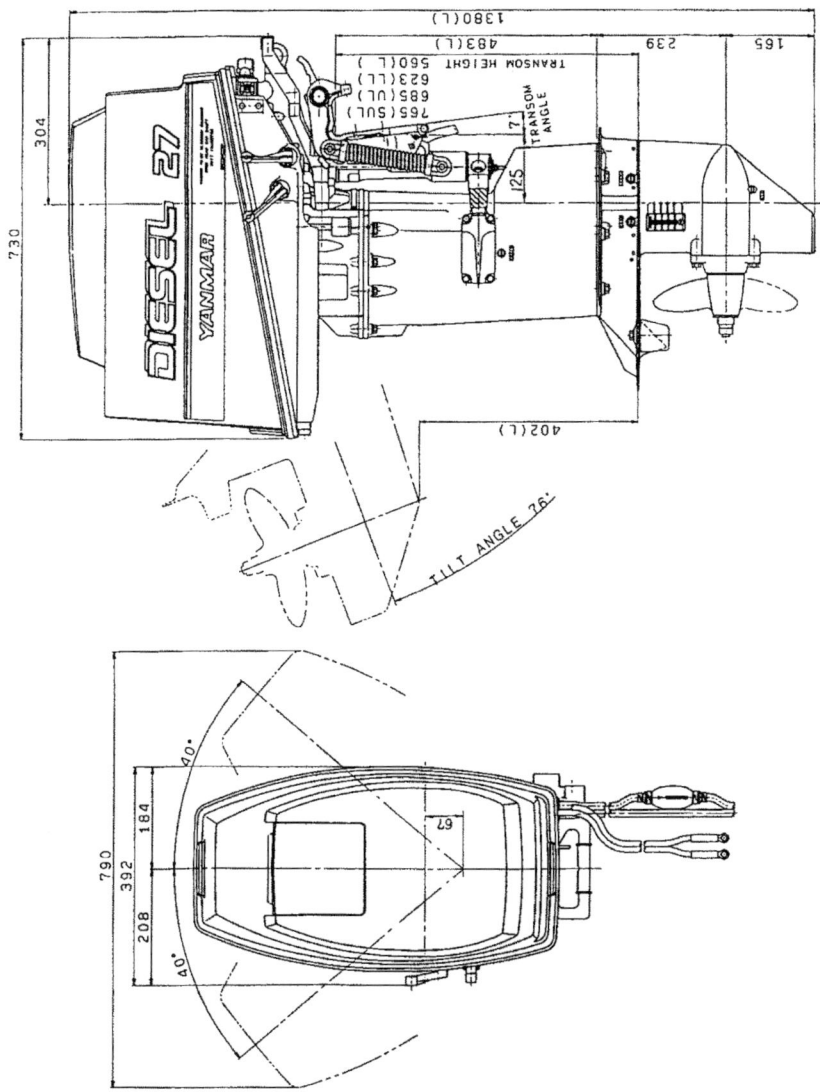

Chapter 1 General
2. Exterior View _____ *SM/D27A & D36A*

(2) D27AXEP

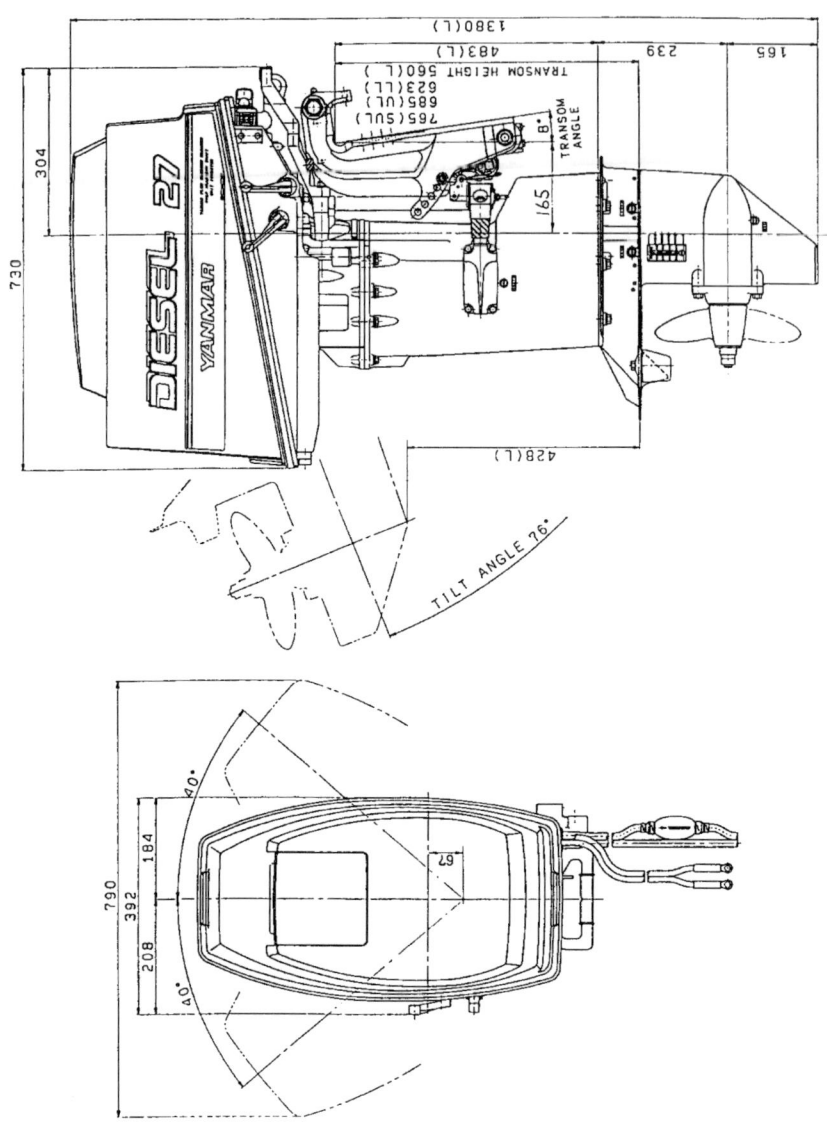

1-4

Printed in Japan
A0A5055-JC03

Chapter 1 General
2. Exterior View

SM/D27A & D36A

(3) D27AYE

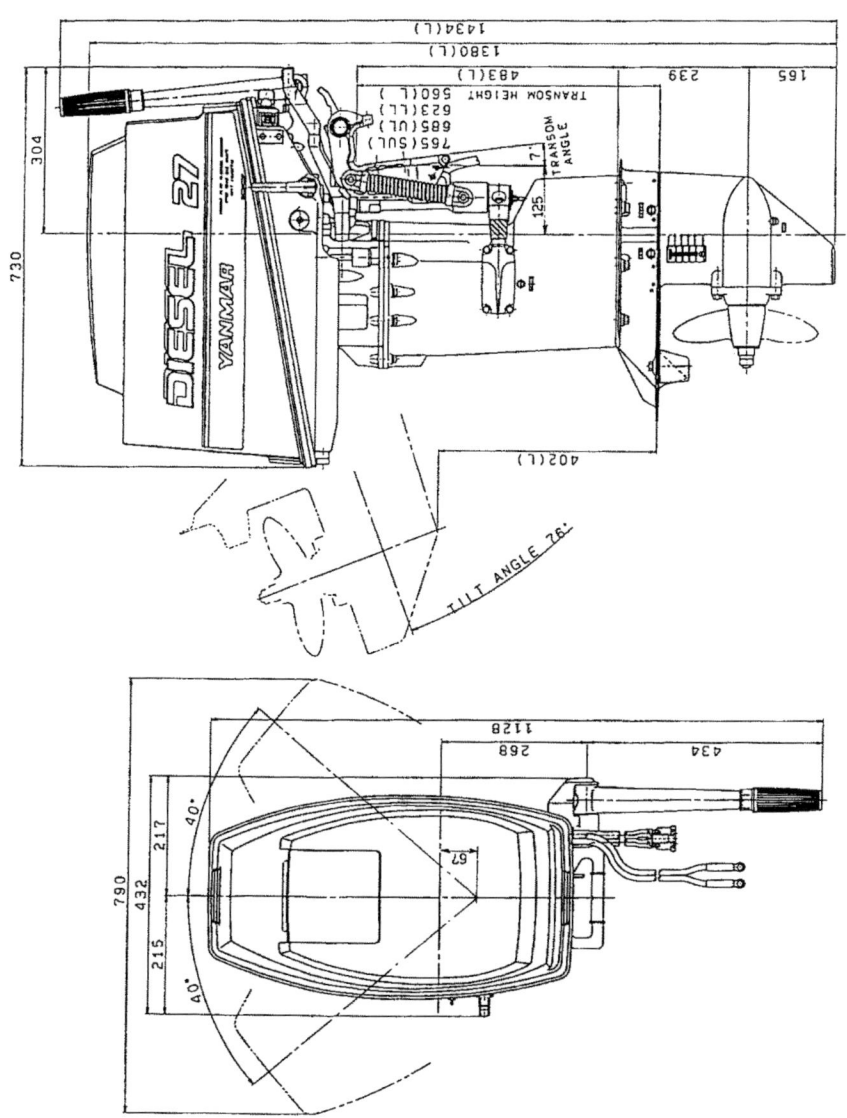

Chapter 1 General
2. Exterior View

_SM/D27A & D36A_

(4) D27AY

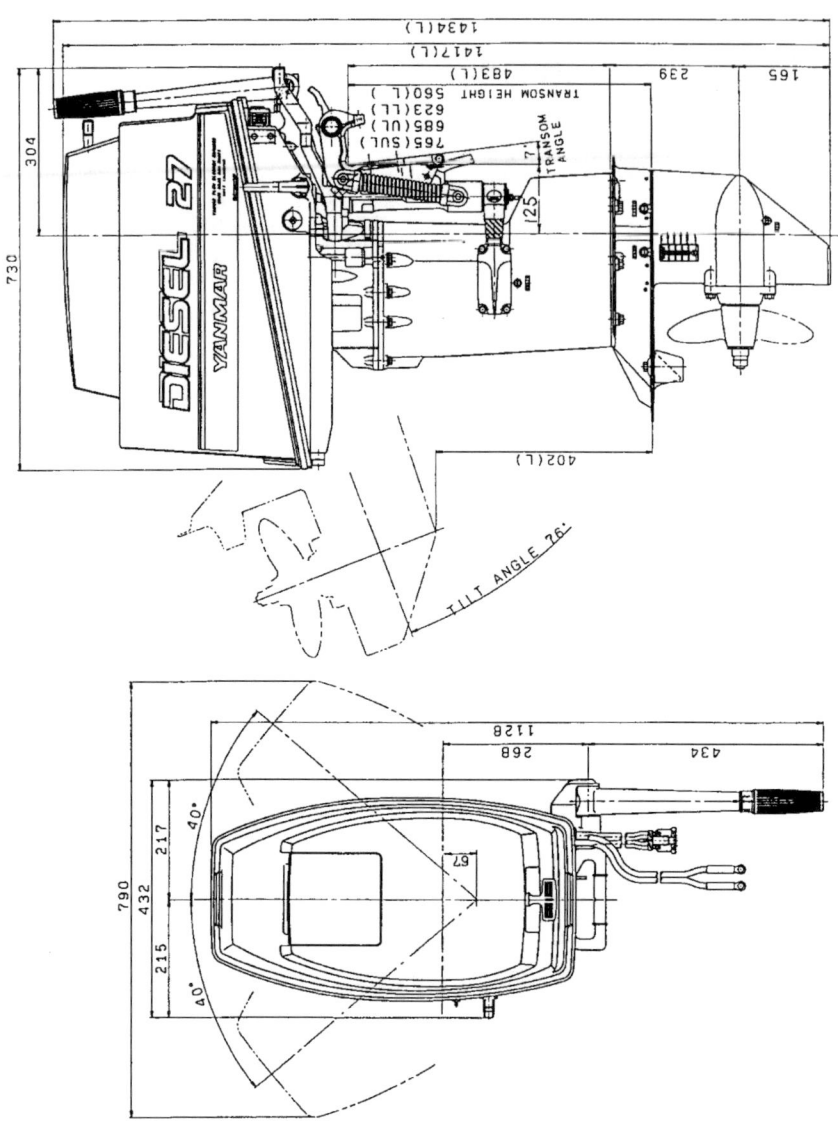

Chapter 1 General
2. Exterior View _____ *SM/D27A & D36A*

2-2 D36A series

(1) D36AX

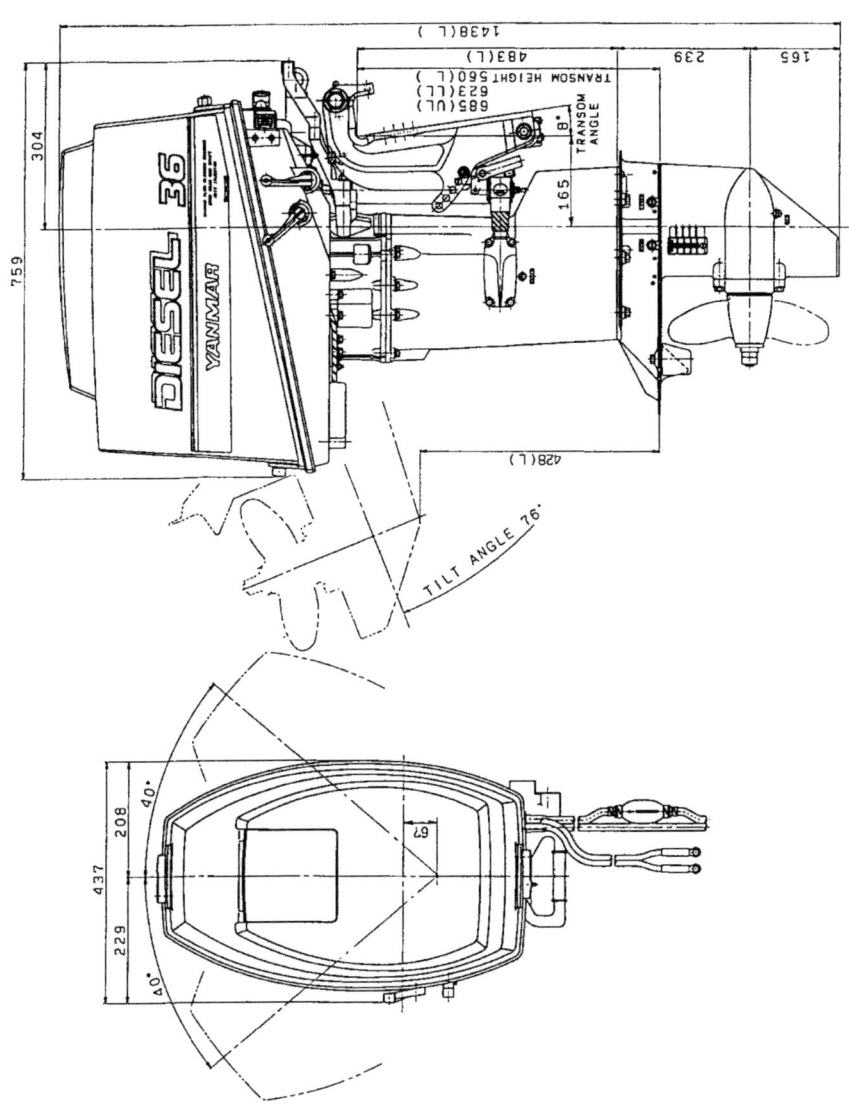

Chapter 1 General
2. Exterior View

(2) D36AXEP

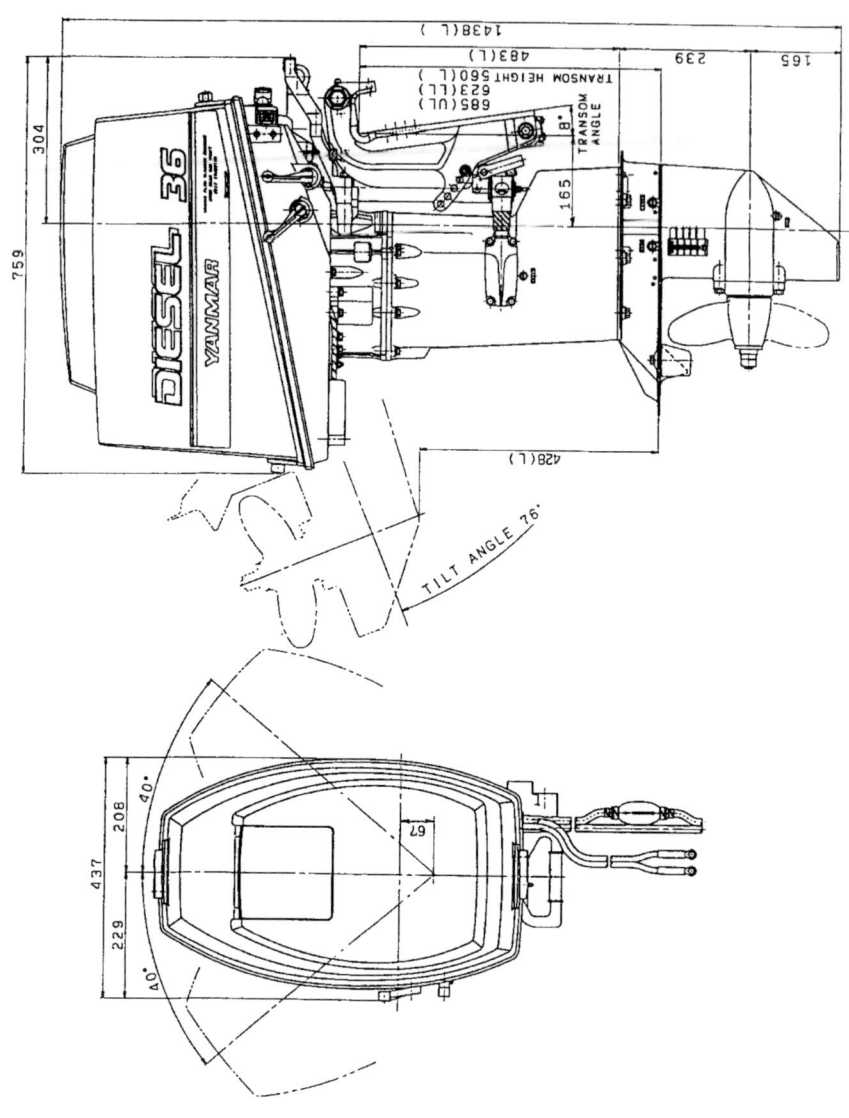

Chapter 1 General
2. Exterior View

(3) D36AY

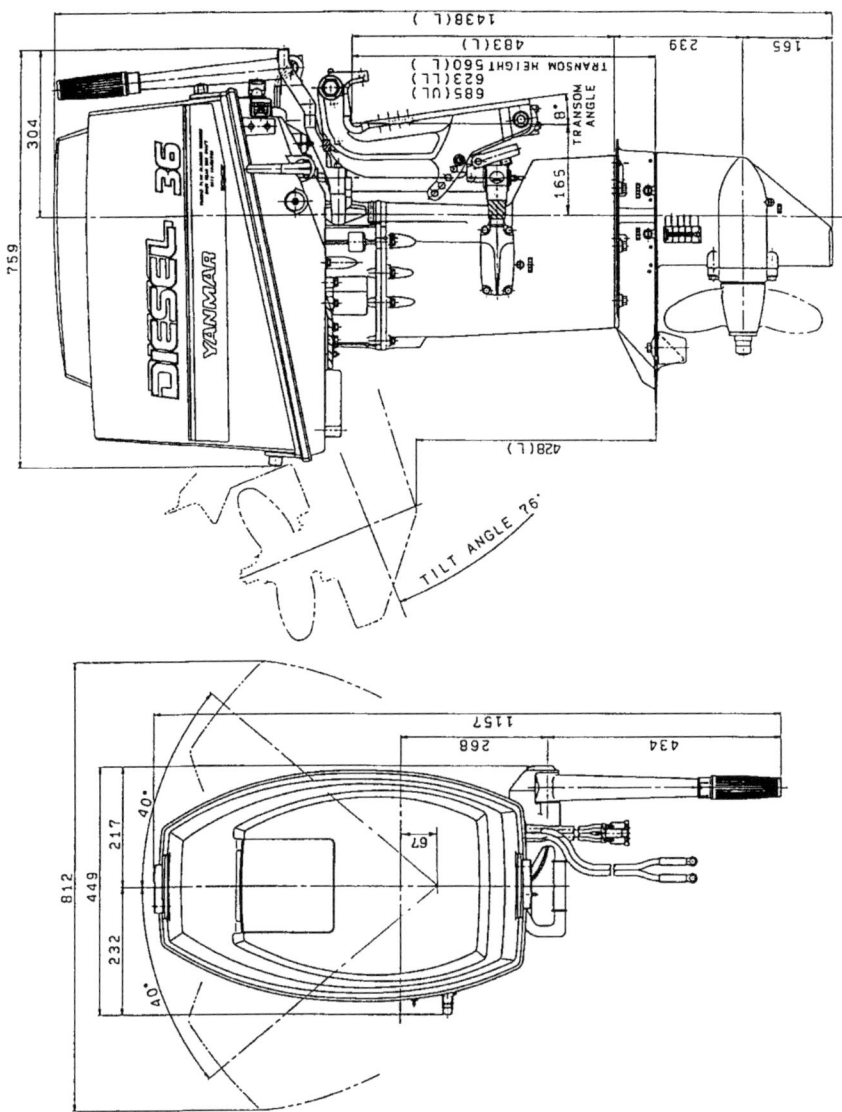

3. Cross-sectional View

(1) D27AX

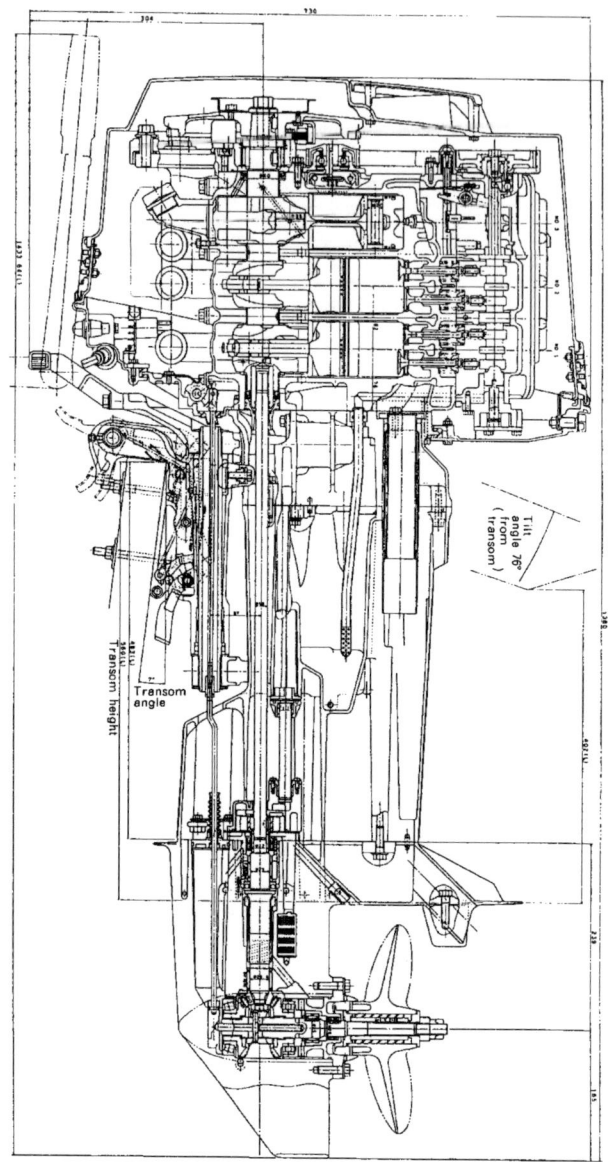

Chapter 1 General
3. Cross-sectional View _____ *SM/D27A & D36A*

(2) D27AY

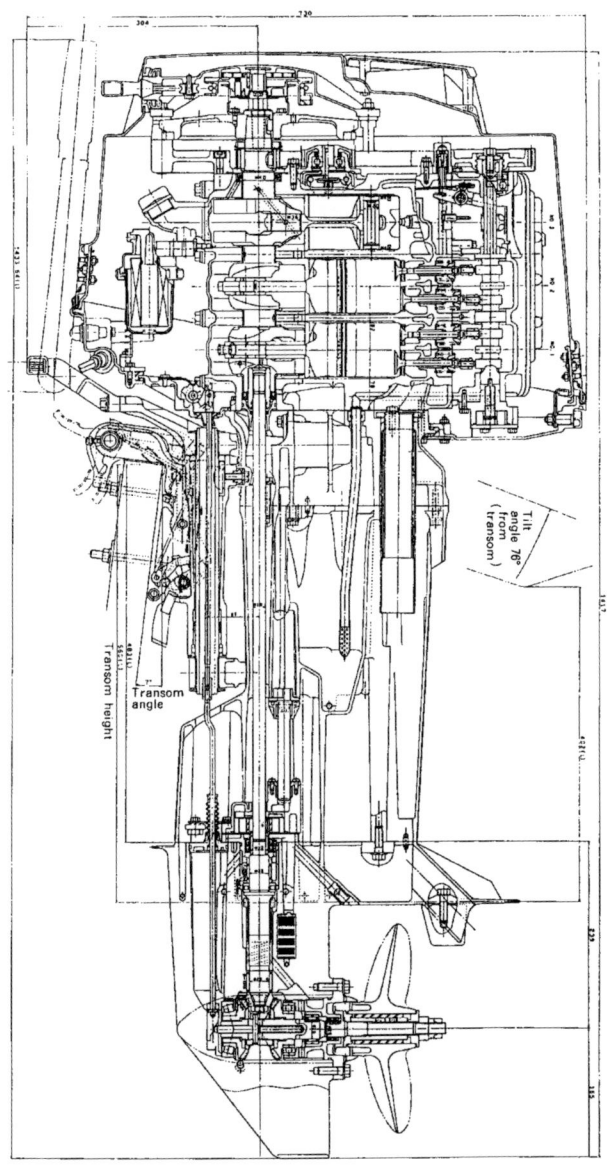

Chapter 1 General
3. Cross-sectional View

SM/D27A & D36A

(3) D36AX

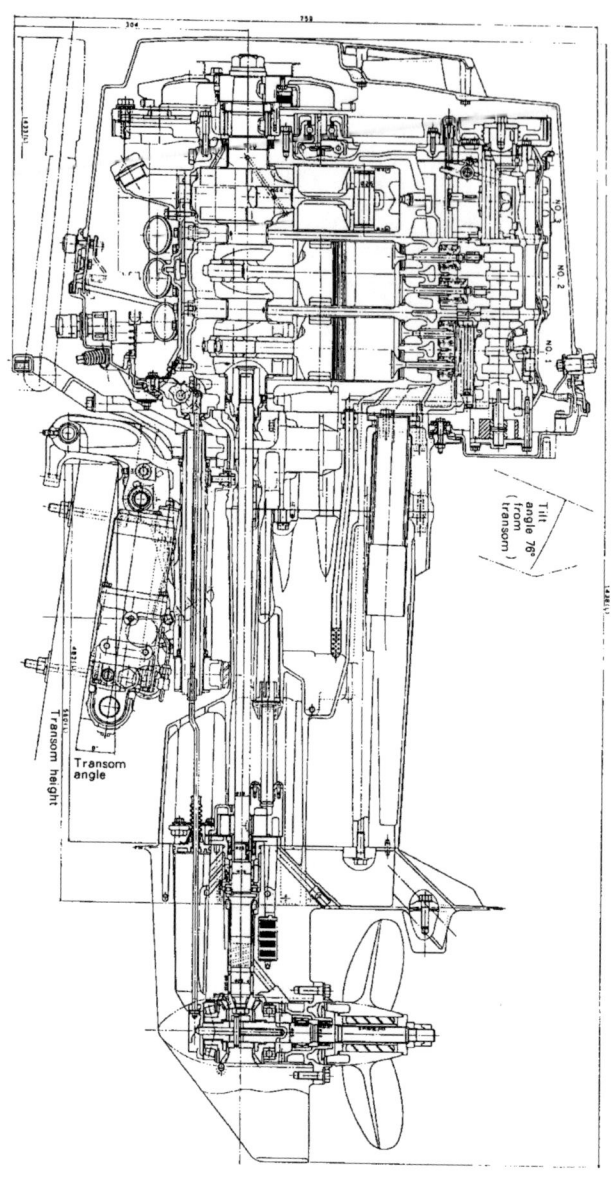

CHAPTER 2
DISASSEMBLY AND REASSEMBLY

1. Preparations Before Disassembly and Reassembly 2-1
2. Tools, Measuring Instruments and Service Equipment 2-2
3. Exploded View of Parts 2-12
4. Reassembly Procedures 2-14
5. Reassembly Procedures for Drive Unit 2-29

1. Preparations Before Disassembly and Reassembly

1-1 Visual symbols for disassembly and reassembly

Visual Mark	Description	Visual Mark	Description
	See	1207B	*1 Apply liquid packing (silicon)
	Caution		Safety
	Measure		Clean
	Oil supply	12	*2 Use torque wrench

*1 Applicable liquid packing:
   THREE BOND 1207B
   THREE BOND 1215 for drive unit
*2 Numeric characters show width across flats.

1-2 Disassembly

(1) Prepare tools, measuring instruments and record sheets.
(2) Prepare the cleaning machine and cleaning vessel.
(3) Prepare a temporary stocking area and container for removed parts.
(4) Drain cooling water and lube oil from the engine.
(5) Put the disassembled parts in order.
(6) The materials and dimensions of bolts and nuts differ from each other. To prevent insertion of wrong bolts or nuts, thread them loosely in their original position after disassembly.
(7) Determine the cause of trouble accurately before disassembly, and do not remove or disassemble unnecessary parts.

1-3. Reassembly

(1) Completely clean the parts, and then check their conditions before reassembly.
(2) Apply new engine oil to sliding parts or moving parts before reassembly.
(3) Replace all gaskets and O-rings with new ones.
(4) Apply the specified liquid packing to the necessary parts to prevent water or oil leakage.
(5) Fit each part while checking oil clearance and thrust clearance.
(6) For parts having match marks, fit the parts by aligning the match marks. Take care of the combination of the parts with selective engagement.
(7) Be sure to use specified bolts, nuts and washers. Tighten the main bolts and nuts to the specified torque. Take special care when tightening aluminum alloy parts.
(8) Apply engine oil to the threads and bearing surfaces of main bolts, and tighten them to the specified tightening torque.

Chapter 2 Disassembly and Reassembly
2. Tools, Measuring Instruments and Service Equipment _____ SM/D27A & D36A

2. Tools, Measuring Instruments and Service Equipment

Although the tools supplied by YANMAR allow you to disassemble or reassemble the main part of an engine, it is recommended to use the following tools and parts for effective and accurate working and correct diagnoses.

2-1. Special tools for disassembly and reassembly (engine side)

No.	Name	Code No.	Description/Usage	Drawing
1	Nozzle opening valve pressure adjusting holder	120270-93010	Nozzle tester, Injection pipe, Adjusting holder assembly	
2	Injector holder	120270-93020		
3	Flywheel removing tool	120270-99850 26116-080754 M8 ×75 3 pcs. 26716-080002 M8 3 pcs	M8 bolt 3pcs. Flywheel removing tool Torque wrench box 22mm	

Printed in Japan
A0A5055-JC03

Chapter 2 Disassembly and Reassembly
2. Tools, Measuring Instruments and Service Equipment
SM/D27A & D36A

No.	Name	Code No.	Description/Usage	Drawing
4	Flywheel fixing lever	120270-99870 26106-080162 M8×16 2pcs.	Fixture	
5	Valve stem seal press-fitting tool	120270-99830	Press-fitting tool Stem seal Valve guide	
6	Unit injector removing lever	120270-99840	Removing lever Push bolt Unit injector	
7	Clearance jig Each jig is for exclusive use	(D27A) 120270-99900 (D36A) 120380-99900	Clearance jig for stator and dynamo wheel	
8	Valve guide removing tool	120270-99770 (D27A) 120270-99790 (D36A) 120380-99790	From inside of cylinder to valve arm case	

Printed in Japan
A0A5055-JC03

Chapter 2 Disassembly and Reassembly
2. Tools, Measuring Instruments and Service Equipment _____ SM/D27A & D36A

No.	Name	Code No.	Description/Usage	Drawing
9	Valve guide press-fitting tool and hand reamer	①120270 -99770 ② (D27A) 120270 -99790 (D36A) 120380 -99790 ③120270 -99780	Positioning of fixing guide which fixes the position of valve guide at the start of press-fitting	1. 3. ⌀D, L D27A 25 45 D36A 30 47.5
10	Valve seat removing tool 120380-99500 (Weld-removing piece) ① (D27A) 120270-99620 (D36A) 120380-99620 ② (D27A) 120270-99630 (D36A) 120380-99630 ③ ④ (D27A) 120270-99460 (D36A) 120380-99460 ⑤ (D27A) 120270-99450 (D36A) 120380-99450		(1) Seat removing rod ③ The end of shaft may be finished with a grinder because it is hardened (HRC47~60) Seat removing rod (An exhaust valve should be installed later at * part) (Reference) (Hardness:Hv279~321 (HRC27~33)) (Material:ø5.5±9.1) Note:1) Install an exhaust valve (120380-11111) later at * part. (2) Weld-and-remove piece. M 6screw Thread depth: Note:1) There must be no return. 2) The dimension of D and H are described in the following table. (Teflon seat and seat removing tool)	Be sure to connect the negative lead of welder here Seat removing rod ③ Weld-and-remove piece ① ② (Disposable) Teflon seat ④ Weld here at three points Teflon seat ⑤

	Name	Dimension H	Dimension D	Remark
①	Weld-and-remove piece(S)	17.5	26.5±0.1	For D27A
②	" (E)	17.5	21.5±0.1	"
①	" (S)	19	32.5±0.1	For D36A
②	" (E)	19	27.5±0.1	"

| 11 | Valve seat press-fitting tool (Cold fitting) 120270-99640 (D27A) 120380-99640 (D36A) Each tool is for exclusive use. | (D27A) ①120270 -99650(S) 120270 -99660(E) ②120270 -99670(S) 120270 -99680(E) | (D36A) ①120270 -99650(S) 120270 -99660(E) ②120270 -996708(S) 120380 -99680(E) | Use liquid nitrogen | 1. 2. |

Chapter 2 Disassembly and Reassembly
2. Tools, Measuring Instruments and Service Equipment   SM/D27A & D36A

No.	Name	Code No.	Description/Usage	Drawing
12	Valve clearance adjusting tool	120270-99860	Screwdriver, Box for valve clearance adjustment, Clearance gauge 0.2 mm	
13	Fuel injection adjusting jig	120270-99800		
14	Adjuster jig	120270-99881	Control lever, Rod, Unit injector, Hexagon rod wrench, Fixing jig	
15	Grease pump	196311-92450		
16	Micrometer		0-25mm 25-50mm 50-75mm	
17	Cylinder gauge		10- 18mm 18- 35mm 35- 60mm 50-100mm	

2-2. Special tools for disassembly and reasembly of lower unit

No.	Name	Code No.	Description/Usage	Drawing
1	Backlash tool (Refer to P.9-1)	196640-92910 Tool 196630-92940 Indicator	Clearance 0.5 ± 0.025, Tool	

Printed in Japan
A0A5055-JC03

Chapter 2 Disassembly and Reassembly
2. Tools, Measuring Instruments and Service Equipment
SM/D27A & D36A

No.	Name	Code No.	Description/Usage	Drawing
2	Indicator plate	196630 – 92960	Dial gauge, Indicator plate, Shim (196630–02801)	
3	Forwarding gear positioning tool 196640–92170 (Refer to P.9-1)	196640 – 92920 196640 – 92870 26636 – 100002 (×2)	Shim (196311–02310)	(10×200)
4	Reversing gear positioning tool 196640–92180 (Refer to P.9-2)	196640 – 92930 26736 – 160002 22137 – 160000 22137 – 240000 26736 – 140002	Shim (196640–02900)	(24) (16) (M16) (M14)
5	Bearing removing tool 196640–92111	196630 – 92510 196630 – 92530 196630 – 92520 26737 – 140002 196640 – 92681 196630 – 92540 22417 – 200160 22137 – 140000		M14
6	Bearing press–fitting tool 196640–92760 (D27A) 196630–92121 (D36A) 196640–92121	①196640–92760 (D27A) ②196640–92771 ③24311–000210 196630–92800 (D36A) ②196640–92771 ③24311–000210		Spacer Only D27A has this spacer

2-6

Chapter 2 Disassembly and Reassembly
2. Tools, Measuring Instruments and Service Equipment
SM/D27A & D36A

No.	Name	Code No.	Description/Usage	Drawing
7	Needle bearing disassembling tool (Oil seal case spacer)	196640-92690 Others are those used as the bearing removing tool		
8	Needle bearing reassembling tool 196640-92140	196640-92610 196640-92620	Drive in	
9	Needle bearing disassembling tool 196640-92160	①196640 -92550 ②196640 -92560 ③196640 -92570 26736-140002 Nut shaft 14 22137-140000 Plain washer 24311-000210 O-ring		
10	Needle bearing reassembling tool	196630-92580 Others are those used as the needle bearing disassembling tool		
11	Oil seal reassembling tool 196640-92760 (D27A) 196630-92131 (D36A) 196640-92131	①196640-92760 (D27A) ②196630-92781 ③196640-92790 (D36A) ②196640-92781 ③196640-92790	Drive in	

Chapter 2 Disassembly and Reassembly
2. Tools, Measuring Instruments and Service Equipment
SM/D27A & D36A

No.	Name	Code No.	Description/Usage	Drawing
12	Thrust bearing inserting tool	196640-92740	Disassembling / Reassembling	
13	Rod cover Spanner (Disassembling tool for power tilting hydraulic cylinder)	196327-92990	L400×W38×H14	
14	Bolt 4 pcs. Nut 1 pc.	Only for D27A 26116-060202 26716-100002	M6×20 For mounting oil seal case M10 For mounting indicator plate	

2-8

Chapter 2 Disassembly and Reassembly
2. Tools, Measuring Instruments and Service Equipment

No.	Name	Code No.	Description/Usage	Drawing
15	Spline sleeve	(D27A) 196630−92950 (D36A) 196640−92950		
16	Forwarding gear reassembling tool set 196640−92080	196640−92810 196640−92830		
17	Reversing gear reassembling tool set 196640−92090			
18	Forwarding/reversing gear disassembling tool 196640−92100	196630−92850 196640−92860 26116−081002 26716−080002		

Chapter 2 Disassembly and Reassembly
2. Tools, Measuring Instruments and Service Equipment

SM/D27A & D36A

No.	Name	Code No.	Description/Usage	Drawing
19	Oil seal reassembling tool (D27A) 196630-92151 (D36A) 196640-92150	(D27A) ①196640-92710 ②196630-92721 ③196630-92731 (D36A) ①196640-92710 ②196640-92720 ③196640-92730 ④196640-92750		

2-3. Gauges for servicing

No.	Name	Code No.	Description/Usage	Drawing
1	Loading	196640-92010	Testing propeller	
2	Stand		For display and repair	
3	Washing joint	196630-92460	Screwed into the lower case when washing. The water port is plugged up.	
4	Tachometer set N1: Engine rpm N2: Tachometer reading N1=60/97×N2(D27A) N1=60/107×N2(D36A)	120270-99250	Measuring instruments: (1) Electromagnetic revolution detector MP-950 (2) Extension cable 5m (3) Digital tachometer HM-620 (Ono Sokki) (4) Mounting angle	
5	Exhaust thermometer set	Thermocouple 120270-99420 Metal fitting 120270-99320	Measuring instruments: (1) Thermocouple (φ1.6CA wire) compensation lead wire length (2) Digital thermometer (3) Spacer hold nut	
6	Nozzle tester	737600-93502	Pressure gauge: 0 ~ 500kgf/cm² Inspect the fuel injection valve for spray shape and injection pressure.	
7	Splash plate	196640-02431(L) 196640-02441(R)	Mount a splash plate on the upper case to keep splashes out during running.	

Chapter 2 Disassembly and Reassembly
2. Tools, Measuring Instruments and Service Equipment   SM/D27A & D36A

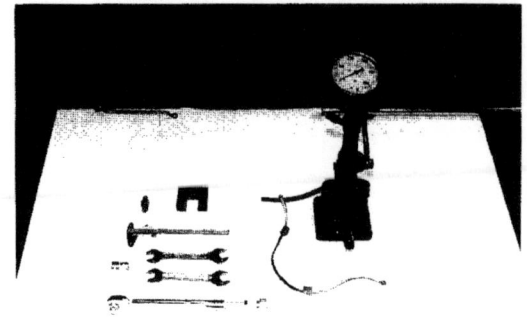

(Nozzle tester, injector holder, etc.)

2-4 Oil, grease, etc. for servicing

No.	Name	Code No.	Description/Usage	Drawing
1	Engine lube oil		CD class 15W40	
2	Lower unit lube oil Lower unit lube oil (in tube)		80W90 (YANMAR's driving gear oil) Insert tube directly into lower case inlet and supply 0.65 ℓ lube oil.	
3	Grease (in tube)		COSMO GREASE DYNAMAX EP No. 2 approximately 200g	
4	Grease		COSMO UREA GREASE 2M Apply it to bearings ranging from drive shaft to crankshaft spline.	
5	Sealant (in tube)		THREE BOND #1215 Apply it to external bolts when screwing them.	
6	Adhesive (in tube)		THREE BOND #1321B For anti-corrosive zinc of lower unit, apply it to upper mount fitting bolts.	
7	Liquid gasket		THREE BOND #1207 (engine) #1215 (Lower part)	
8	Super screw lock	977778 – 00010	Powerful adhesive to fix bolts semi-permanently. 50g	
9	Repairing paint (engine coating)	TOR – 90720003	YANMAR Blue Gray-M	Cowling
		TOR – 90710003	YANMAR Medium Gray-M	Lower case
10	Repairing gasket mover spray		PANDO-391D (THREE BOND) Be careful when using it, because it might damage painting around gasket and causing rust.	

Chapter 2 Disassembly and Reassembly
3. Exploded View of Parts

SM/D27A & D36A

3. Exploded View of Parts

(1) Engine parts

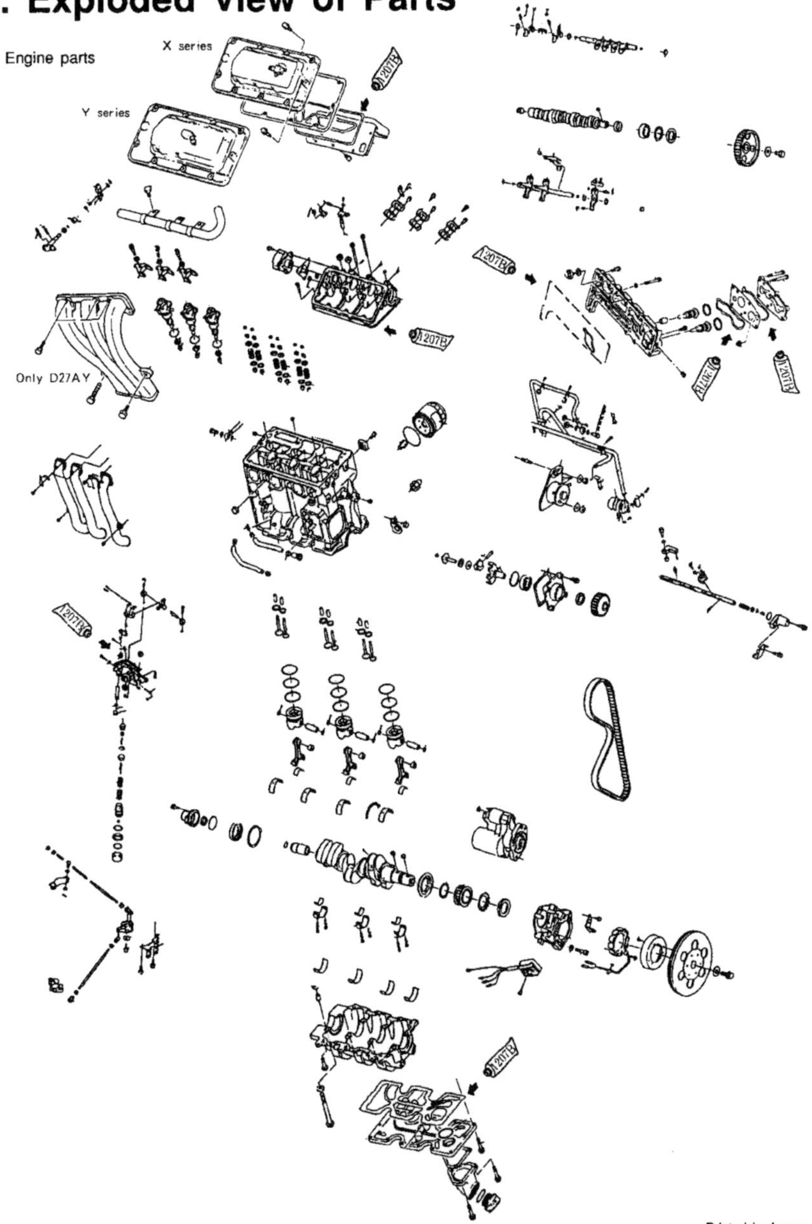

X series

Y series

Only D27AY

Chapter 2 Disassembly and Reassembly
3. Exploded View of Parts

SM/D27A & D36A

(2) Drive unit parts

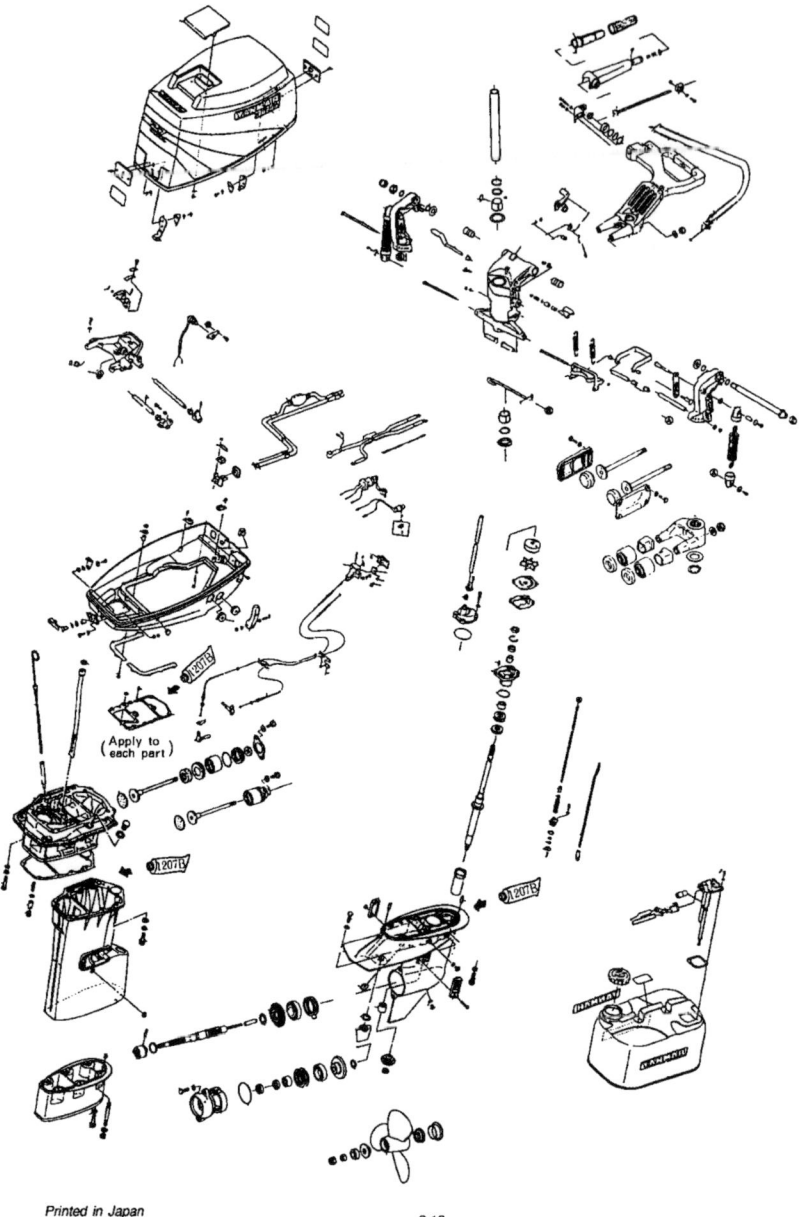

4. Reassembly Procedures

No.	Item	Procedure	Symbol	Photo/Diagram
1	Cylinder block	Clean carefully the inside of the cylinder block and each hole.		
2	Reversing cylinder block	Place the cylinder block with side cover facing upward.		
3	Side cover	1) Install the anti-corrosive zinc to the side cover. Anti-corrosive zinc tightening torque: 0.8~1.0 kgf-m 2) Install the side cover. Bolt M6×20 5 pcs. M6×40 5 pcs. M6×50 1 pc. Side cover tightening torque: 0.8~1.0 kgf-m (Use liquid packing)	10	(Apply the liquid packing) (Install the side cover)

4	Thermostat and Jiggle valve	1) Supply approximately 200cc of oil.
		2) Install the thermostat to the side cover.
		Thermostat:
		  Valve opening temp.: Exhaust temp. 65 ℃ / Water temp. 72 ℃
		  Valve full-open temp.: Exhaust temp. 75 ℃ / Water temp. 82 ℃
		M6×50 4 pcs.
		3) Install the jiggle valve to the side cover.
		4) Install the thermostat cover.
		Bolt M6×25 2 pcs.
		M6×50 5 pcs.
		Cover tightening torque: 0.8~1.0 kgf-m
		— Note: —
		1. Use new packing and seal washers.
		2. Take care not to install a wrong thermostat. The exhaust temp. thermostat differs from the water temp. thermostat.
		(Use liquid packing)
		Do not forget to apply thermostat cover packing.
			1207B
			10
			⚠
			1207B
				(Install the thermostat to the side cover)
				Apply yellow paint on bolt's head after air is removed from oil case.
				Jiggle valve
				Water temp. thermostat / Exhaust temp. thermostat / Supply lube oil through this part.
				(Install the thermostat cover)

2-14

Chapter 2 Disassembly and Reassembly
4. Reassembly Procedures
SM/D27A & D36A

No.	Item	Procedure	Symbol	Photo/Diagram
5	Reversing cylinder block	Place the cylinder block with the valve arm case side facing down. (Use a wooden stand.)		
6	Intake/exhaust valve	Insert the intake/exhaust valve into the cylinder block using a magnetic rod.		(Install the intake/exhaust valve with a magnetic rod)
7	Piston and Connecting rod	1) Assemble the piston and connecting rod, and set the stopper ring. (Match the recess and the embossed mark on the rod.) 2) Insert the piston and connecting rod assembly into the cylinder block from the crankshaft side. The recess side should come from the flywheel side. (Repeat the same procedures for other two cylinders.) 3) Install the crank pin metal (upper part). Note: 1. When inserting the piston, make sure that the piston ring gaps are apart from each other at equal distance. 2. Apply lube oil to the piston outside surface and the crank pin metal.	⚠ 🛢	(Install the connecting rod)

Printed in Japan
A0A5055-JC03

2-15

Chapter 2 Disassembly and Reassembly
4. Reassembly Procedures   _SM/D27A & D36A_

No.	Item	Procedure	Symbol	Photo/Diagram
8	Crankshaft and main bearing	1) Install the main bearing (upper, with oil groove and oil hole) to the cylinder block. 2) Install the thrust metal A (circular) and the oil seals (upper and lower) to the crankshaft, and install the crankshaft to the cylinder block. 3) Install the thrust metal B (semi-circular). Note: 1. Apply lube oil fully before assembling. 2. Check that there is no dust or flow on the rear surface of the bearing before reassembling.	⚠ 🛢	(Set the crankshaft)

9	Rod metal cap	1) Draw near the connecting rod to the crankshaft.
		2) Install the crank pin metal (lower) to the rod metal cap. Install the rod metal cap to the connecting rod, and tighten the rod bolts at the specific tightening torque.
		   M7 (D27A) 6pcs.
		   M9×43 (D36A) 6pcs.
		
		Rod bolt tightening torque (kgf-m): 2.35 ± 0.15 D27A / 4.75 ± 0.25 D36A
		
		Note:
		1. Check the alignment mark.
		2. Apply lube oil to the threads and the seat of the rod bolts before tightening.
		3. Tighten the bolts diagonally to prevent tightening stress.
			⚠
			
			🛢
			
			🔧 12
				(Set the rod metal cap)

10	Main bearing case and main bearing (lower)	1) Install the main bearing (lower) to the main bearing case. 2) Apply the sealant (THREE BOND #1207 B) to the main bearing case joint. 3) Install the main bearing case assembly to the cylinder block. Metal cap bolt tightening torque: 4.8 ± 0.2 kgf-m M10 8pcs. D27A / 8.0 ± 0.5 kgf-m M12 8pcs. D36A Auxiliary bolt tightening torque M8 12 pcs.: 2.5~2.7 kgf-m Note: 1. Set the knock bush before installing the main bearing case assembly. 2. Apply lube oil to the threads and the seat of the metal cap bolts before tightening. 3. Install the oil cooler to the main bearing case in advance. (D36A)	⚠ 🛢 1207B 🔧 12 🔧 14	(Set the main bearing (lower)) (Tighten the metal cap bolt)

Chapter 2 Disassembly and Reassembly
4. Reassembly Procedures
_SM/D27A & D36A_

No.	Item	Procedure	Symbol	Photo/Diagram
		4) Check the crankshaft thrust clearance. 	Crankshaft thrust clearance	0.11~0.39mm D27A
	0.146~0.454mm D36A | 5) Install the oil seal case assembly on the side opposite to the flywheel. Bolt M6×16 1pc. | Oil seal case tightening torque	0.8~1.0kgf-m | 6) Install the O-ring (1AP16) to the spline piece. —Note:— 1. Use new oil seal and O-rings. 2. Apply plenty of grease to the oil seal and install the oil seal with care. 7) Install the flywheel side oil seal.	⊋ ⊊⃗10	(Measure the thrust clearance) (Install the oil seal)
11	Belt pulley	1) Install the key. 2) Install the belt pulley. 3) Install a crown washer as a stopper. 4) Tighten a crown nut. | Crown nut tightening torque	M35	17±0.5 kgf-m D27A
	M42	18±0.5 kgf-m D36A | 5) Fully bend the crown washer. 6) Install the key.	⊊⃗	(Tighten the crown nut) (Install the key)

Chapter 2 Disassembly and Reassembly
4. Reassembly Procedures   *SM/D27A & D36A*

No.	Item	Procedure	Symbol	Photo/Diagram

12	Starting motor bracket	1) Knock 2pcs. of parallel pins (6×10) into the cylinder block.
		
		2) Align the starter bracket with the positioning parallel pins (6×10), and install the starter bracket.
		  Bolt M8×25 1pc.
		  Bolt M8×45 3pcs.
		
		   | Bracket tightening torque | 2.5~2.7 kgf-m |
		
		3) Install the indicator plate (with a lift metal fitting).
		  Bolt M8×16 1pc.
		
		   | Metal fitting tightening torque | 2.5~2.7 kgf-m |
			⌀12	(Install the bracket)

13	Fuel feed pump	Position the fuel pump assembly to the stud bolts (M8×18), and fix the assembly temporarily with M8 nuts and washers. (Adjust belt tension with the adjusting nuts when installing a bolt, and tighten the M8 nuts.)		(Install the fuel feed pump)

14	Handle mount assembly unit	1) Install the handle mount assembly by aligning it with the positioning spring pin (4.0A ×8).
		  Bolt M6×20 5pcs.
		
		   | Handle mount tightening torque | 0.8~1.0 kgf-m |
		
		Note:
		1. Apply lube oil to the 1st, 2nd and 3rd governor lever assemblies and regulator assembly before installation.
		2. For connecting the 2nd and 3rd governor lever assemblies with the control rod, refer to 3-25
		3. Be sure to attach correctly the stop rings and the link stoppers to the joints of the governor lever.
			⌀10	(Install the handle mount assembly)

2-18

Printed in Japan
A0A5055-JC03

Chapter 2 Disassembly and Reassembly
4. Reassembly Procedures
_____SM/D27A & D36A

No.	Item	Procedure	Symbol	Photo/Diagram
15	Stem seals and Valve spring	1) Knock the stem seals into the cylinder block. (Use a special tool) *Note:—* *The intake and the exhaust stem seals are not interchangeable. D36A (Intake stem has white painted mark.)* 2) Set the valve spring retainers, the valve spring and the stoppers, and install the cotters. (The valve spring is double spring.) 3) Measure the top clearance. (Measure the top clearance)		(Knock the stem seal with a jig) (Install the cotter with a spring press jig)
16	Control rod and stop lever	1) Install the control rod to the cylinder block. 2) Install the 3rd lever pin to the control rod. 3) Install the standard pin to the control rod. 4) Install the control rod rail to the cylinder block. Bolt M6×16 1pc. 	Rail tightening torque	0.8~1.0kgf-m	 5) Install the adjuster to the control rod. Hexagonal hole bolt M4×18 3pcs. 6) Install the start spring to the control rod. 7) Install the start spring cover. Bolt M6×25 2pcs. 	Cover tightening torque	0.8~1.0kgf-m	 Complete the procedure 1) to 7) before installing the valve arm case according to procedure No.21 (Valve arm case).	10	(Set the control rod) (Set the start spring cover)

Printed in Japan
A0A5055-JC03

Chapter 2 Disassembly and Reassembly
4. Reassembly Procedures _____*SM/D27A & D36A*

No.	Item	Procedure	Symbol	Photo/Diagram
17	Unit injector	1) Knock the positioning spring pin into the cylinder block. 2) Set the O-ring, packing, and protector to the unit injector. 3) Install the unit injector assembly surely, aligning it with the positioning spring pin. (Insert the unit injector so that the fork adjuster pin matches up.) Hexagonal hole bolt M8×35 3pcs. Unit injector tightening torque: 2.6~2.8kgf-m —Notes:— 1. Check that there is no foreign substance in the unit injector insertion hole. 2. Use new protector and O-ring for the unit injector. 3. Before inserting the unit injector, apply molybdenum disulfide to the O-ring. 4. Be careful of the direction of the washer. (The spherical side of the washer should contact with the injector stopper.) 5. Remove carbon or other contamination from the nozzle injection hole.	6 ⚠ 🖌	(Set the protector) (Install the unit injector)
18	Stop lever and valve arm case	1) Install the stop lever to the valve arm case. 2) Install the return spring. —Notes:— 1. Use new O-ring (1AS20, 1AP7.0) and boot. 2. Apply lube oil to each part before reassembling. 3) Install a pin to the stop lever. 4) Knock the stopper parallel pin (3×28) into the stop lever. 5) Install the intake/exhaust valve arm and the valve arm shaft spring to the valve arm case together with the valve arm shaft. (Note that the No.1 exhaust valve arm has a seat for the decompression lever.) 6) Install the fuel injection valve arm together with the valve arm shaft. 7) Knock the blind caps into the holes A and B on the top and the bottom. (D27A···16–4pcs D36A···16–2pcs, 22–2pcs)	⚠ 🖌 10	(Valve arm shaft) Flywheel side — This part does not accept bolt M10 bolt can be inserted here for removal. Insert bolts into these 4 cuts (Shaft turning stopper). Each of intake/exhaust valve arm shaft and FO valve arm shaft has 4 cuts, but their positions differs. (Install the injection valve arm and the valve arm shaft)

Printed in Japan
A0A5055-JC03

Chapter 2 Disassembly and Reassembly
4. Reassembly Procedures

SM/D27A & D36A

No.	Item	Procedure	Symbol	Photo/Diagram
		Notes: 1. Apply lube oil to the valve arm and the valve arm shaft joint before reassembling. 2. Check that the blind plugs are firmly tightened at both ends of the valve arm shaft. 3. Align the cuts of the valve arm shaft with the valve arm case bolt holes when inserting the valve arm shaft. 4. For easy insertion, screw a M10 bolt into the valve arm shaft.		

19	Camshaft and pulley	Install the following to the valve arm case :
		1) Set the bearing (6006) to the camshaft.
		2) Install the camshaft from the flywheel side.
		(Insert the outer race until it reaches the innermost surface.)
		3) Install a spacer and an oil seal.
		4) Install the timing belt cover.
		  Bolt M6×12 4 pcs.
		
		| Oil seal retainer tightening torque
			0.8~1.0 kgf-m |
			
			Note:
			1. When installing the bearing and the oil seal, apply lube oil to the joint.
			2. When installing the pulley, take care not to damage the oil seal lip.
			
			5) Install the key first and then the pulley to the camshaft, and tighten the bolts.
			  Bolt M10×25 1 pc.
			
			| Pulley tightening torque
				4.5~5.0 kgf-m |
				
				(Tighten the cam pulley at the hexagonal seat (46 wide).)
						(Camshaft and pulley)
						
						(Lube oil pump)

20	Lube oil pump	1) Install the lube oil pump drive shaft to the groove of the camshaft. Bolt M6×60 4 pcs. | Lube oil pump tightening torque	0.8~1.0 kgf-m | **Notes:** 1. Use new packing. 2. Apply grease between the lube oil pump drive shaft and the camshaft.		(Valve arm case assembly)

Chapter 2 Disassembly and Reassembly
4. Reassembly Procedures

No.	Item	Procedure	Symbol	Photo/Diagram
21	Valve arm case	1) Set two knock bushes. 2) Apply liquid packing. Install the valve cap on top of valve and install the assembly to the cylinder block. (Apply grease to the valve cap). Bolt M6×35 4pcs. M8×20 8pcs. Valve arm case tightening torque: M6 0.8~1.0kgf-m / M8 2.5~2.7kgf-m *Note:* 1. Align the punched marks on the timing belt cover and the pulley.	⚠ ⌐10 ⌐12 1207B	(Apply liquid packing to the valve arm case assembly) (Install the valve arm case)
22	Governor	1) Install the governor assembly. Bolt M6×25 4pcs. Cover tightening torque: 0.8~1.0kgf-m *Notes:* 1. Apply lube oil to the bearing and the governor weight. 2. Check that the governor weight and spindle move smoothly. Also check that the split pin (2.0×10) is properly installed to the governor weight pin, and is bent.	⌐ ⚠ 🛢	(Governor)

2-22

Chapter 2 Disassembly and Reassembly
4. Reassembly Procedures
SM/D27A & D36A

No.	Item	Procedure	Symbol	Photo/Diagram
23	Engine control device	1) Install the remote control cable bracket. Bolt M6×16 2pcs. Bracket tightening torque: 0.8~1.0kgf-m 2) Install the regulator lever assembly. Bolt M6×16 1pc. Lever tightening torque: 0.8~1.0kgf-m 3) Install the regulator rod (with joint and spring). Handle mount—regulator lever nut M5 Rod tightening torque: $0.45^{\pm 0.05}$ kgf-m	8 10	Bracket, Regulator lever, Regulator rod, Reverse rod, Regulator lever (Control device)
24	Oil filter, pressure control valve and hydraulic switch	1) Install the filter fixing bolt to the cylinder block. 2) Install the oil filter. 3) Install the pressure control valve and the hydraulic switch. (Hydraulic switch) D27A : 0.2kgf/cm² D36A : 0.5kgf/cm²		Oil filter, Hydraulic switch, O-ring, Fixing bolt, Lube oil pressure control valve (Installation position of oil filter, etc.)

2-23

Chapter 2 Disassembly and Reassembly
4. Reassembly Procedures — SM/D27A & D36A

No.	Item	Procedure	Symbol	Photo/Diagram

25	Fuel filter and fuel pipe	1) Install the fuel filter to the cylinder block.
		Binding Small screw
		M5×14 1pc.
		
		2) Install the fuel pipe.
		• Fuel pipe (1)
		  FO feed pump − bottom cowling
		• Fuel pipe (2)
		  FO feed pump − FO filter
		• Fuel pipe (3)
		  FO filter − cylinder block (Install a pipe joint.)
		• Fuel pipe (4)
		  Cylinder block − bottom cowling (Install a pipe joint.)
		
			Pipe joint bolt M12 tightening torque	1.5∼2.5kgf-m

Fuel pressure control valve M12 tightening torque	1.5∼2.5kgf-m	 ―Notes:― 1. Use new seal washers. 2. Fasten the piping firmly with a hose clamp. 3. Install anti−vibration stays.	⌒17	(Install the feed pump) (Fuel pipe) Starter fixing bolt
26	Oil filler	1) Install the oil filler to the main bearing case. M6×30 2pcs. M6×45 1pc. 	Oil filler tightening torque	0.8∼1.0kgf-m	 2) Install the oil filler cap. (Set an O-ring.)	△ ⌒10	(Bracket) (Regulator)
27	Starting motor	Install the starting motor. Bolt M12×45 2pcs. | Starting motor tightening torque	8.0$^{\pm 0.5}$ kgf-m | Install the regulator. M6×20 2pcs. | Regulator tightening torque	0.8∼1.0kgf-m		⌒17	(Starting motor) (Install the starting motor)

Chapter 2 Disassembly and Reassembly
4. Reassembly Procedures
_____SM/D27A & D36A

No.	Item	Procedure	Symbol	Photo/Diagram

28	Flywheel, generator and timing belt	1) Install the timing belt (Z=101⋯D27A, Z=111⋯D36A) to the stator assembly, and install the assembly to the starter bracket.
		Bolt M6×40 3pcs.
		
		| Stator tightening torque
			0.8~1.0kgf-m |
			
			2) Install the dynamo wheel to the flywheel.
			Bolt M6×10 3pcs.
			
			| Dynamo wheel tightening torque
				0.8~1.0kgf-m |
				
				Apply screw lock to the bolts in 1) and 2)
				
				3) Adjust the belt tension by positioning the fuel feed pump, and tighten the nuts.
				
				| Nut (M8) tightening torque
					2.5~2.7kgf-m |
					
					Note:
					  As for adjusting the timing belt, refer to p.3-29.
					
					4) Install the flywheel (with dynamo wheel).
					
					| Tightening torque
						17±0.5 kgf-m M16 D27A	28±1.0 kgf-m M24 D36A |
							
							Check that the stator and the dynamo wheel do not contact.
							Clearance jig 120380-99900 D36A
							             120270-99900 D27A
							Notes:
							  1. Apply lube oil to the tapered part of the flywheel and the threads and the seat of the flange bolt.
							  2. The nut (M24×1.5) is threaded clockwise.
							  3. Use the flywheel fixing lever.
								⚠
								
								🛢
								
								🔧 10
								🔧 12
								🔧 22
									(Install the timing belt)
									Nut
									Flywheel
									
									Dynamo wheel
									Generator
									Stator
									Distance piece
									Ⓐ
									Ⓑ

29	Intake pipe	1) Install the intake pipe.
		Bolt M6×16 3pcs.
		     M6×20 6pcs.
		
			Intake pipe tightening torque	0.8~1.0kgf-m	
					
					Notes:
					  Check that there is no foreign substance inside the intake pipe before installing.
					
					2) Install the cooling pipe on the oil cooler cover side (Only D36A).
						⚠
						
						🔧 10
							Ⓑ Ⓐ
							Only D27AY
							(Intake pipe)

Chapter 2 Disassembly and Reassembly
4. Reassembly Procedures

No.	Item	Procedure	Symbol	Photo/Diagram
30	Valve arm case cover	1) Adjust the valve arm clearance and the injection timing. *Note:* As for adjusting the valve arm clearance and the injection timing, refer to p.3-15, and 3-16. 2) Install the valve arm retainer to the unit injector valve arm. Bolt M6×12 3pcs. | Valve arm retainer tightening torque	0.8~1.0kgf-m | 3) Install the valve arm case cover assembly to the valve arm case. Bolt M6×20 9pcs. | Cover tightening torque	0.8~1.0kgf-m		1207B 10	(Valve arm cover) D27AX D36AX D27AY D36AY

31	Connecting engine with drive unit	1) Place the drive unit on the stand. (As for connecting the bottom cowling with the upper case, refer to p.4-6.)
		2) Set the LO intake pipe, packing, O-ring and seal rubber to the top of the upper case, and install the engine.
		(To set the engine, use the lift metal fitting together with the drive shaft spline piece.)
		Connect the engine with the upper case, aligning to the positioning parallel pins (6×12).
		Bolt M8×25 2pcs.
		     M8×30 3pcs.
		     M8×55 6pcs.
		
			Connection tightening torque	2.5~2.7kgf-m	
					
					Note:
					Apply grease (COSMO UREA GREASE 2M) to the fitting spline. Take care of the wiring, piping and linkage for being enfolded when connecting the engine.
						⚠
						12
							(Engine)
							
							(Connection)

Chapter 2 Disassembly and Reassembly
4. Reassembly Procedures

No.	Item	Procedure	Symbol	Photo/Diagram
32	Wire harness and battery cable	1) Connect the wire harness and the battery cable. Insert terminals for wiring connections. 2) Connect the decompression wire and the regulator wire. 3) Install the reverse rod. 4) Make sure that there is no obstacle around the engine. (Refer to the wiring diagram on p.6-6 ~ 6-10.) 5) Connect the pipe coming from the cylinder block and the FO feed pump to the FO connector of the bottom cowling.		Power tilt motor Ⓐ / Ⓑ, Red, Black, Blue, Red, Green, Relay box, Blue, Red, Green, Switch Power tilt specification for LEP, LLEP and ULEP (Connect the wire harness) (Adjust the regulator) (Clamp the piping) (The view after completing the handle mount)

Chapter 2 Disassembly and Reassembly
4. Reassembly Procedures

No.	Item	Procedure	Symbol	Photo/Diagram
33	Top cowling	1) Install the top cowling. 2) Tighten the bolts with a clamp handle.		(Top cowling)
34	Fuel oil pipe	Connect the fuel oil pipe. (Tank – engine) Tighten the hose bands securely. Be careful of the hose direction. (The priming pump should be on the right.)	D27AX D36AX D27AY D36AY	(Fuel oil tank and fuel oil pipe)

2-28

Chapter 2 Disassembly and Reassembly
5. Reassembly Procedures for Drive Unit

SM/D27A & D36A

5. Reassembly Procedures for Drive Unit

No.	Item	Procedure	Symbol	Photo/Diagram
1	Lower gear case (Refer to p.4-9)	1) Insert the needle bearing (BH-1616) into the lower gear case. 2) Install the zinc. Apply screw lock (THREE BOND 1321B) to the bolts. 3) Insert the needle bearing (HK2520) into the oil seal case. 4) Insert the needle bearing (RNA-4904R) into the bearing housing. Insert the oil seal so that the outside of the oil seal comes to the outside. Installing direction (The spring should face to the seawater side) Drive in ↓ Tool / Tool / Tool (Inserting oil seal) 5) Insert the ball bearing (6008) into the reverse gear. 6) Insert the shim into the bearing housing, and insert the reverse gear assembly. (For easy reassembling, heat the bearing housing to 50°C~60°C.) 7) Insert the taper bearing (30207) into the forward gear.	1207B	Drive in ↓ Tool ↓ Oil seal case / Tool (Bearing housing) (Install the reverse gear assembly)

Printed in Japan
A0A5055-JC03

2-29

Chapter 2 Disassembly and Reassembly
5. Reassembly Procedures for Drive Unit
SM/D27A & D36A

No.	Item	Procedure	Symbol	Photo/Diagram
		8) Install the dog clutch to the propeller shaft. (Apply grease to the shift plunger before installing.) Shift plunger — Dog clutch Stop ring Cross pin Shift spring (Propeller shaft) The dog clutch has 6 claws on forward side, 3 claws on reverse side. Install the reverse collar (standard 2.6). 9) Insert the propeller shaft assembly into the bearing housing. (Do not forget to install the reverse collar.) 10) Install the thrust bearing to the drive shaft. (Heat the side which contacts the drive shaft flange to 80°C before installing.) 11) Install the oil seal case to the drive shaft. (Do not forget to install the thrust bearing shim.) 12) Insert the shim into the lower gear case, and insert the outer race.		Pin — Shift plunger Cross pin ring — Propeller shaft — Shift spring Dog clutch (Spring and dog clutch) (Insert the outer race) (Press and fit the outer race)

Chapter 2 Disassembly and Reassembly
5. Reassembly Procedures for Drive Unit

_SM/D27A & D36A_

No.	Item	Procedure	Symbol	Photo/Diagram
		13) Insert the oil guide as shown in the photo. Insert the shift rod into the lower gear case. (Apply grease to the O-rings. Apply bond 1215 to the bolts.) Face the cut of the shift to the propeller side. 14) Install the drive shaft assembly to the lower gear case. 15) Install the drive shaft and the pinion gear. | Tightening torque M12 × 1.25	9.5 ± 0.5 kgf-m | Position the pinion gear. (Refer to p.9-1.) Clearance 0.5 ± 0.025 mm (Reference) A 0.1 shim takes away 7/100 backlash. Remove the pinion gear and the drive shaft after measuring. 16) Insert the forward gear. Set the pinion gear, and insert the drive shaft assembly.		(Insert the oil guide) (Install the shift cam) (Measure the drive shaft) (Adjusting and measuring)

Chapter 2 Disassembly and Reassembly
5. Reassembly Procedures for Drive Unit

No.	Item	Procedure	Symbol	Photo/Diagram
		17) Install the propeller shaft assembly.		
		18) Measure the propeller shaft thrust clearance. (Refer to p.4–14.) Use the standard collar for the forward side, and adjust the clearance at the reverse gear collar (standard 2.6).		
		19) Adjust the forward gear backlash. (Refer to p.4–12.)		
		20) Adjust the reverse gear backlash. (Refer to p.4–12.)		
		21) After adjusting the backlash, insert the oil seal into the oil seal case. (The spring side should face to the seawater side.) (Apply seawater-resistive grease to the lip which surface contacts sea water. Do not forget to install an O-ring.)		(Install the bearing housing)
		22) Insert two O-rings into the bearing housing. (Apply grease to the O-ring and seawater-resistive grease to the oil seal lip.)	1207B	
		23) Install the bearing housing to the lower gear case. Apply THREE BOND 1215 to the bolts before installing.		
		M10×35 tightening torque : $3.8^{\pm 0.1}$ kgf-m		
		24) Knock 2 knock pins (6 × 12) into the oil seal case, and install the packing outer plate.	14	(Measure the backlash)
		25) Install the wood ruff key to the drive shaft.		
		26) Install the cooling water pump assembly. Apply grease to the O-ring so that the O-ring does not fall out. When inserting, match up the key groove to the drive shaft. Apply THREE BOND 1215 to the fixing bolt.		(Drive shaft)

Chapter 2 Disassembly and Reassembly
5. Reassembly Procedures for Drive Unit _____ SM/D27A & D36A

No.	Item	Procedure	Symbol	Photo/Diagram
		27) Install 3 drain plugs. 28) Install the water inlet cover. *(diagram: Water inlet cover, Drain plug, Gasket, Water inlet cover, Gasket Drain plug)*		(Install the cooling water pump)
2	Upper case (Refer to p.4–5.)	1) Apply liquid packing to the separate engine mount, and install the separate engine mount to the upper case. 2) Insert the exhaust pipe and the packing. (Apply THREE BOND 1215 to the fixing bolts.) | M6×20 tightening torque	0.7~0.9kgf-m | 3) Install the seal rubber. 4) Install the mount rubber. | M8×60 tightening torque	1.9~2.1kgf-m | 5) Install the drain plug (1 pc.). (Install the seal rubber)	🔧 12 🔧 14 1207B	(Engine mount) (Lower part of upper case)

2-33

Chapter 2 Disassembly and Reassembly
5. Reassembly Procedures for Drive Unit _____*SM/D27A & D36A*

No.	Item	Procedure	Symbol	Photo/Diagram
3	Clamp bracket (Refer to p.4-4.)	1) Set O-rings to the tilt tube hole. (Fit the small O-ring to the inside and the large O-ring to the outside.) (Reference) There is a cast indication on the manual valve hole. <table><tr><td>Tilt tube nut tightening torque</td><td>2.0kgf-m</td></tr></table>		(Clamp bracket)
4	Swivel bracket (Refer to p.4-1~4-3)	1) Insert 2 bushes into the tilt tube hole of the swivel bracket. (Face the groove to the grease hole.) 2) Set a washer to the right of the tilt lock lever, and install the tilt lock lever to the swivel bracket. Set a washer, a spring, a washer and a tilt collar to the right of the tilt lock lever. Set a washer to the left of the tilt lock lever, install the tilt lock lever to the swivel bracket, and fasten the swivel bracket with a split pin. (Fix the left and right lock levers.) 3) Insert 2 bushes for fixing hydraulic cylinder. 4) Insert a bush into the hydraulic cylinder.		(Swivel bracket) (Insert bushes for fixing hydraulic cylinder)

2-34

Printed in Japan
A0A5055-JC03

Chapter 2 Disassembly and Reassembly
5. Reassembly Procedures for Drive Unit

SM/D27A & D36A

No.	Item	Procedure	Symbol	Photo/Diagram
4-1	Manual tilt swivel bracket (D27A)	Procedures 1) to 4) are the same as the swivel bracket. 5) Install clamp brackets (left and right) to the swivel bracket with a tilt tube. (Do not forget to install a tilt spacer, a tilt lever and a tilt lever spring in advance.) 6) Assemble the tilt lock lever. 7) Install the tilt assist to the clamp bracket. 8) Install the tilt assist spring and the cover. 9) Set bushes, springs and collars to the tilt lock lever (left and right), and install the tilt lock lever to the swivel bracket. (Do not forget to install a tilt spring, hook and lever.)		

Chapter 2 Disassembly and Reassembly
5. Reassembly Procedures for Drive Unit
SM/D27A & D36A

No.	Item	Procedure	Symbol	Photo/Diagram
4-2	Manual tilt swivel bracket with shock absorber (D36A)	Procedures 1) to 4) are the same as the swivel bracket. 5) Set a washer to the tilt lock lever (left), and insert the tilt lock lever. 6) Set a tilt stop lever (with spring pin), a tilt spring hook, a return spring and a tilt lock collar to the tilt lock lever (left). Set a washer to the tilt lock lever (right), insert it, and fix the tilt lock levers (left and right) with a split pin. 7) Install a rubber grip to the tilt lock lever. 8) Install a tilt lever bolt to the tilt spring hook. 9) Install 2 bushes to the swivel bracket. 10) Set a bush to the shock absorber, and install the shock absorber to the swivel bracket. 11) Set a return spring lever to the change lever of the return spring and the shock absorber. (Set the return spring lever) 12) Insert a swivel bracket pin into the swivel bracket, and install gas shock. 13) Install a washer and a stop ring to both sides of the swivel bracket pin.		(Insert 2 bushes into the swivel bracket) (Set the return spring lever)

Chapter 2 Disassembly and Reassembly
5. Reassembly Procedures for Drive Unit

SM/D27A & D36A

No.	Item	Procedure	Symbol	Photo/Diagram
		14) Install the tilt lever to the gas shock change lever.		
		15) Set the tilt stop rod to the tilt stop lever, and install the tilt stop lever to the tilt lever fitting bolt.		
		16) Install springs to the swivel bracket pin and the tilt lever.		
		17) Install the half tilt spring hook to the swivel bracket.		
		18) Knock the spring pin into the swivel bracket.		(Install the tilt lever)
		19) Set the half tilt stopper to the spring pin.		
		20) Set the half tilt arm to the spring pin. Set 2 collars and 2 washers, and tighten with bolt nut (both sides).		
		21) Install the half tilt spring to the half tilt arm and the tilt spring hook.		
		22) Install a rubber grip to the half tilt arm.		(Tilt stop rod and spring)

(Shock absober)

Swivel bracket

Handle bracket

Steering bracket

Swivel bracket

Tilt tube

Clamp bracket

Thrust rod

Support bolt

Support cylinder

Bush

Bracket lower mount

(Manual tilt swivel bracket for D36A)

Printed in Japan
A0A5055-JC03

2-37

Chapter 2 Disassembly and Reassembly
5. Reassembly Procedures for Drive Unit
SM/D27A & D36A

No.	Item	Procedure	Symbol	Photo/Diagram

4-3	Hydraulic tilt swivel bracket (option)	Procedures 1) to 4) are the same as the swivel bracket.
		
		5) Fix the hydraulic cylinder with pins. Fasten the both sides with washers and stop ring.
		
		6) Set 2 collars to the hydraulic cylinder rod side of the swivel bracket.
		
		7) Install the cylinder support to the hydraulic cylinder fixing side.
		
		8) Install 4 grease nipples.
		
		9) Install one clamp bracket (manual valve side) to the outboard motor mount by tightening the bolts. In addition, install the swivel bracket and then the other clamp bracket.
		
		10) Install the cylinder support with nuts.
		
		11) Install the tilt tube, in which 2 washers are inserted, and fix with nuts.
		
		   Tightening torque: 2 kgf-m
		
		Tighten the cylinder support nuts fast.
		
		   M16 tightening torque: 11~15 kgf-m
		
		Install the tilt tube cap. (Too much tightening damages the tilt tube cap because it is made of plastic.)
		
		12) Install the power unit to the clamp bracket. (Apply THREE BOND 1215 to the bolts.)
		
		   Tightening torque: 2 kgf-m
		
		13) Pass through the clamp bracket grommet hole, and fix it with a grommet. (Use a rubber grommet cut with a scissor)
			32
			
			24
			
			14
				(Fix the hydraulic cylinder)
				
				(Insert 2 washers into the tilt tube)
				
				(Install the power unit)
				
				(Cut the rubber grommet and insert it)

Chapter 2 Disassembly and Reassembly
5. Reassembly Procedures for Drive Unit

SM/D27A & D36A

No.	Item	Procedure	Symbol	Photo/Diagram
		14) Install 4 flare adapters attaching a seal tape. (2 adapters for the hydraulic cylinder and 2 adapters for the power unit)		
		3/16 tightening torque — 1.1kgf-m		
		15) Install the flare tube, and adjust it so that it does not contact with any part.		
		16) Install the thrust rod.		(Install the thrust rod)

Chapter 2 Disassembly and Reassembly
5. Reassembly Procedures for Drive Unit

SM/D27A & D36A

No.	Item	Procedure	Symbol	Photo/Diagram
5	Bottom cowling (Refer to p.4-6.)	1) Install the bottom cowling (with a FO connector, a stop wire, a key switch, a LO warning lamp, a battery cord, 2 grommet brackets) to the engine mount. Tighten the collar, the grommet and the washer with united bolts. | Tightening torque	0.8kgf-m | Note: Insert washers if the bolts are tightened on aluminum body. 2) Install the holder A to the bottom cowling. (harness) (The holder A fixing screw is tapping screw, and the washer is made of plastic.)		(Collar, grommet and washer)
6	Shift bracket (Refer to p.4-7.)	1) Install the shift rod to the detent with a shift rod pin, and fix it with a washer and a split pin. 2) Install the detent and the shift shaft, and fix it with a spiral roller pin. 3) Install the safety lever, and fix it on the shift shaft with a spiral roller pin. 4) Install the reverse limit shaft to the reverse lever with a spiral roller pin. 5) Install the detent spring A and B. (Apply grease to the detent springs.) 6) Install the shift bracket (stop bracket for D27A) assembly to the engine mount. 7) Install the bottom cowling to the engine mount. As for D27A, push seal rubber with a pushing plate. As for D36A, tighten the grommet with bolts and nuts.		(Install the shift bracket (stop bracket for D27A) assembly) (Shift bracket (stop bracket for D27A) assembly)

Chapter 2 Disassembly and Reassembly
5. Reassembly Procedures for Drive Unit

SM/D27A & D36A

No.	Item	Procedure	Symbol	Photo/Diagram
7	Steering handle, etc (Refer to p.4-16)	1) Sandwich the wave washer between washers, insert a bush and install the steering handle. M8×25, M8×55 (applied with THREE BOND 1215) Insert the bush in the steering handle and fix it with the handle support. 2) Install the grommet to the regulator cable, and set the assembly to the bottom cowling. 3) Install the steering brake to the swivel bracket. (Install a spring, a rubber and a washer with a set bolt.)		(Wave washer) (Steering brake)
8	Setting lower and upper gear case	1) Knock 2 knock pins into the lower gear case. (Apply THREE BOND 1215 to the pins.) 2) Fit the extension for the LL and UL models. (Apply THREE BOND 1215 to the whole installation surface.) 3) Insert the cooling water pipe into the cooling water outlet side of the lower gear case. Note: Attach water seal rubbers on the upper and lower side of the cooling water pipe before inserting the pipe. 4) Insert the water seal rubber into the upper case, fix the rubber with the seal rubber case, and install the lower gear case. M10×35 Tightening torque 3.8kgf-m 5) Install the connection. 6) Connect the shift rod and the shift cam using the connector. Set both at the reverse condition, and tighten them with nuts.	(LL) (UL) ⚠ 🔧 14 1207B	(SUL For D27A only)

		L	LL	UL	SUL
Drive shaft	D27A	196630-04500	196631-04500	196632-04500	196633-04500
	D36A	196640-04051	196641-04051	196642-04051	—
Shim assembly		196630-02801			
Extension		—	196641-02530	196642-02530	196643-02530
Bolt		—	196640-10710	196630-10330	
Nut		—	196640-10070	—	
Washer			196630-10390		
Parallel pin		—	196630-10530		
Shift cam		196640-06552	196641-06551	196642-06551	196643-06550
Cooling water pipe		196640-08550	196641-08550	196642-08550	196643-08550

Chapter 2 Disassembly and Reassembly
5. Reassembly Procedures for Drive Unit _____ SM/D27A & D36A

No.	Item	Procedure	Symbol	Photo/Diagram
9	Bracket	1) Insert a plate into the pivot shaft, and set the upper and lower bushes. (The lip sides of the upper and lower bush should face the inside.) Install the upper and lower washers. (Apply grease to the washers.) Plate — Seal, Bush, Washer / Bush, Seal, Washer 2) Insert the pivot shaft. 3) Install the bracket mount to the lower side of the pivot shaft. (Do not forget to install the rubber damper.) Warm the bracket damper before inserting it. Insert it with a bolt nut, and fix it with a washer and a stop ring. 4) Install the upper case assembly to the swivel bracket assembly. | Tightening torque	3.8kgf-m | Attach stopper and a washer (applied with screw lock) to the bolt, and tighten it. The lower side should be tightened with a washer and a nut. The upper side should be tightened with no stopper and screw lock. Insert a screwdriver into the rubber side to fix the bolt when tightening. 5) Install the bracket handle. (Apply THREE BOND 1207B.) 6) Install the lower mount housing. (Apply THREE BOND 1207B.) (Tighten the bracket(lower side))	14 17 1207B	(Insert the upper and lower bush) (Insert the pivot shaft) (Bracket of the upper side of the upper case) (Install the upper case assembly)

2-42

CHAPTER 3

INSPECTION AND SERVICE PROCEDURES FOR ENGINE PARTS

1. Inspection and Service Procedures for Engine Parts 3-1
2. Cylinder Block 3-2
3. Piston and Connecting Rod 3-4
4. Crankshaft 3-7
5. Camshaft 3-8
6. Cylinder Head 3-9
7. Valve Arm Case 3-13
8. Intake/Exhaust Valve Arm and Unit Injector 3-14
9. Thermostat 3-17
10. Unit Injector 3-18
11. Governor 3-24

1. Inspection and Service Procedures for Engine Parts

1-1 Do the following procedures before inspection and service of main parts :

(1) Clean all parts completely to remove dust, oil, carbon and scale, etc.
(2) Blow compressed air through oil holes to remove deposit and check that there is no clogging.
(3) Remove carbon deposited on the cylinder head and the intake/exhaust valve, etc. with care so that the parts will not be damaged.
(4) Put in order the parts that have a definite combination to prevent confusion.

1-2 Standard for replacing (repairing) parts

Measure each part and check it according to the respective inspection procedures. If the part is defective or exceeds the wear limit, replace it.
Also replace any part which is expected to exceed the wear limit by the next inspection even if it is within the wear limit now.

2. Cylinder block

The cylinder block integrates the cylinder head, the cooling water jacket and the crank case. The exhaust manifold is housed inside, and the cylinder liners are cast in the cylinder block.

1. Cautions when reassembling and servicing

    (1) Provide high pressure steam cleaning to the inside of the cylinder block, the cylinder head and each oil hole.
    (2) Knock 2 knock bushes into the top of the cylinder head.
    (3) Replace the old anti-corrosive zinc.

2. Cylinder liner
    The cylinder liners are cast in the cylinder block. They employ the direct seawater cooling system.

    (1) Cautions when reassembling and servicing

        1) Check the inside surface of the cylinder liner, and measure the inside diameter of the liner. Repair the part according to reboring (oversize of 0.25) if it exceeds the size limit.

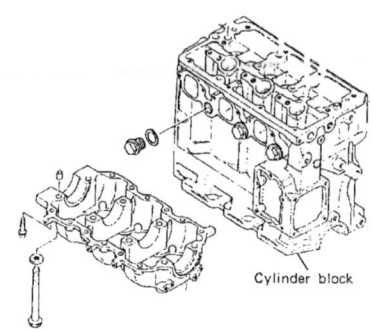

Cylinder block

(mm)

		Standard	Wear limit
Liner inside diameter	L	φ70 +0.030 (φ82) +0.020	
	M	φ70 +0.020 (φ82) +0.010	70.10 (82.10)
	S	φ70 +0.010 (φ82) 0	

( ) for D36A

(Cylinder block)

Chapter 3 Inspection and Service Procedures for Engine Parts
2. Cylinder Block
SM/D27A & D36A

3. Main bearing and main bearing case

- The main bearing is a 4-point bearing aluminum metal. The thrust bearing consists of circular at upperside and full-circular at lowerside.
- The main bearing case, which comes in a monoblock is connected and tightened to the cylinder block at the center of the crankshaft. The oil cooler is installed in place of the bottom lid. (Oil cooler is for D36 only)

(1) Cautions when reassembling and servicing

1) Install the main bearing, and tighten the main bearing case to the specified tightening torque. Measure the inside diameter of the main bearing, and replace it if it exceeds the wear limit.

D27A

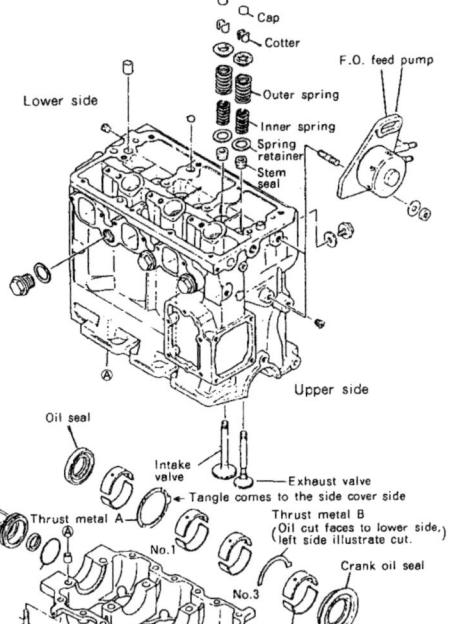

(mm)

	Standard	Wear limit
Main bearing inside dia.	$\phi 40^{+0.026}_{+0.010}$	40.1
Cap bolt (M10) tightening torque	Head width (14) $4.8^{\pm 0.2}$ kgf-m	

D36A

(mm)

	Standard	Wear limit
Main bearing inside dia.	$\phi 50^{+0.037}_{+0.010}$	50.1
Cap bolt (M12) tightening torque	Head width (17) $8.0^{\pm 0.5}$ kgf-m	

(Main bearing case)

3. Piston and Connecting Rod

- The piston is of cast aluminum. A wear-resistant ring is provided to the 1st ring groove, and the cherry blossom shaped combustion chamber is molded on the piston crown.
- The piston rings consist of the two compression rings and one oil ring.
- The piston pin is full floating type.
- The connecting rod is stamped and has I-shaped stem with the large connecting rod end split horizontally.
- The crank pin metal is provided with a thin aluminum backing.

1. Cautions when reassembling and servicing

    (1) Piston head and combustion surface
    Remove the carbon deposit on the piston head and combustion surface. Take care not to damage the piston. Check that there is no flaw on the combustion surface.

    (2) Measurement of piston outside diameter
    - Measure the piston outside diameter, and check the wear of the ring grooves. If the size measured is below standard, or if they are excessively damaged, replace the piston.
    - Measure the piston outside diameter 20mm above the piston bottom and at a right angle to the piston pin.

    (3) Replacement of piston pin
    - The fitting size of the full floating type piston pin is shown below.
    - Apply oil to the pin, and insert it into the pin hole at normal temperature (when the piston is replaced).

(mm)

	Standard	Wear limit
Piston outside diameter L	φ69.940 +0.015 (φ81.95)+0.005	69.88 (81.88)
Piston outside diameter M	〃 ±0.005	69.88 (81.88)
Piston outside diameter S	〃 −0.005 −0.015	69.88 (81.88)

(L, M or S is punched on the piston head) ( ) for D36A

(mm)

	D27A	D36A
Piston pin hole inside diameter	φ20 +0.008 / 0	φ26 +0.009 / 0
Piston pin outside diameter	φ20 0 / −0.009	φ26 0 / −0.013

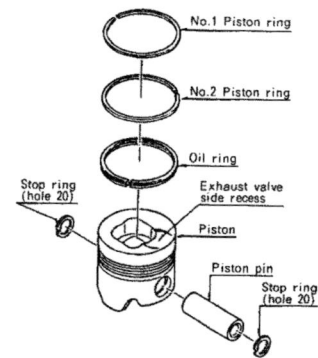

Chapter 3 Inspection and Service Procedures for Engine Parts
3. Piston and Connecting Rod

SM/D27A & D36A

(4) Measurement of piston ring
Measure the width and thickness of the piston rings, clearance between the ring groove and the ring end gap. If they exceed the wear limit, replace the ring. Handle the rings with care because the SUS nitride rings are brittle.

1) Measurement of thickness and width of piston ring

(mm)

		Standard	Wear limit
No.1 Piston ring	Thickness	$2.75^{\pm0.10}$	—
	Width	$1.5^{-0.010}_{-0.025}$ $(2.0^{-0.010}_{-0.025})$	—
No.2 Piston ring	Thickness	$3.1^{\pm0.10}$	—
	Width	$1.5^{-0.010}_{-0.025}$ $(2.0^{-0.010}_{-0.025})$	—
Oil ring	Thickness	$2.2^{\pm0.20}$	—
	Width	$3.5^{-0.010}_{-0.025}$	—
No.1 ring and groove clearance		0.050~0.080	0.12
No.2 ring and groove clearance		0.030~0.060	0.12
Oil ring and groove clearance		0.020~0.050	0.12

( ) for D36A

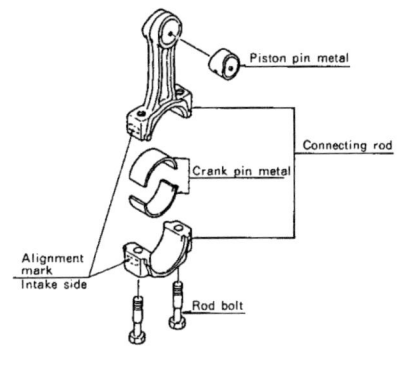

Piston pin metal
Connecting rod
Crank pin metal
Alignment mark
Intake side
Rod bolt

2) Measurement of piston ring end gap
Insert the piston ring into the ring gauge. Measure the piston ring end gap with the gauge.

(mm)

	Standard	Wear limit
End gap of No.1, No.2 piston ring	0.25~0.35 (0.25~0.40)	1.2
End gap of oil ring	0.15~0.35	1.2

( ) for D36A

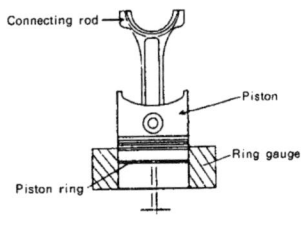

Connecting rod
Piston
Ring gauge
Piston ring

(Measurement of ring end gap)

3) Replacement of piston ring
Fully clean the ring groove when replacing the ring. For fitting, the side with the maker's punched mark at the end gap should be at the top. Check that the ring can be moved lightly.

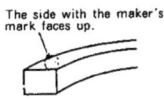

The side with the maker's mark faces up.

(Fitting direction of ring)

Chapter 3 Inspection and Service Procedures for Engine Parts
3. Piston and Connecting Rod

2. Connecting rod

(1) Cautions when reassembling and servicing

1) Measurement of distortion and parallelism of large and small end hole.
   Put the lips through the large and small end holes of the connecting rod and measure the distortion and parallelism of the connecting rod. Replace it if the size deviates from the standard.

(mm)

	Standard	Wear limit
Parallelism	0.05 (For 100mm)	0.07 (For 100mm)

(2) Measurement of inside and outside diameter of piston pin and metal

1) Check the piston pin and metal for the seizure, cracks and other damages. Replace it if excessively damaged.
2) Measure the inside diameter of the piston pin metal. Replace it if they exceed the wear limit.

(mm)

	Standard	Wear limit
Piston pin outside diameter	$\phi 20 \, {}^{0}_{-0.009}$ ($\phi 26 \, {}^{0}_{-0.013}$)	19.90 (25.90)
Piston pin metal inside diameter	$\phi 20 \, {}^{+0.038}_{+0.025}$ ($\phi 26 \, {}^{+0.038}_{+0.025}$)	20.10 (26.10)
Clearance between piston pin and metal	0.025~0.047 (0.025~0.051)	0.1

( ) for D36A

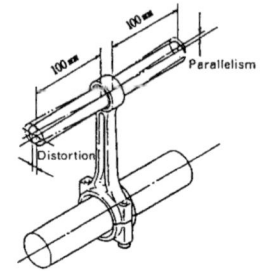

(Measurement of distortion and parallelism)

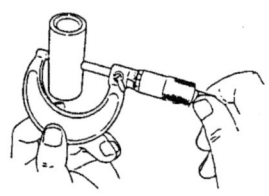

(Measuring piston pin)

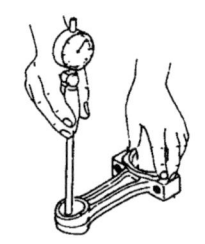

(Measuring piston pin metal)

Chapter 3 Inspection and Service Procedures for Engine Parts
4. Crankshaft _____*SM/D27A & D36A*

4. Crankshaft

- The crankshaft is stamped, and comes in a monoblock with the balancer.
- The spline piece is press-fitted to the power take-off (bottom end).

1. Cautions for reassembling and servicing

   (1) Inspection of crankshaft
   Fully clean the crankshaft. Check it for damages with a color checker or a magnetic flaw detector. If it is damaged excessively, replace it. If the damages are light, repair the crankshaft.

   (2) Measuring crankshaft distortion
   Support the crankshaft journals by V-blocks at both end, turn the crankshaft and measure the deviation of the middle journal with the dial gauge.

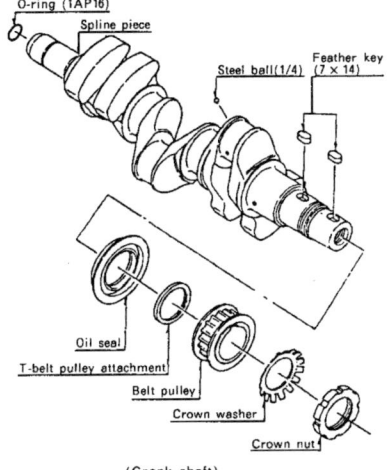

(Crank shaft)

(mm)

	Standard	Wear limit
Crankshaft distortion	<0.03	0.05

   (3) Measuring crankshaft pin and journal
   Measure the outside diameter of the crankshaft pin and the journal. If the wear (roundness or taper degree) is excessive, either replace or repair. When the outside diameter is within the wear limit, consider to be adjustable.

(mm)

		Standard	Wear limit
Pin	Shaft outside diameter	$\phi 36 \begin{smallmatrix}0\\-0.015\end{smallmatrix}$ ($\phi 44 \begin{smallmatrix}0\\-0.015\end{smallmatrix}$)	35.90 (43.90)
	Rod metal inside diameter	$\phi 36 \begin{smallmatrix}+0.042\\+0.020\end{smallmatrix}$ ($\phi 44 \begin{smallmatrix}+0.046\\+0.024\end{smallmatrix}$)	36.08 (44.08)
	Oil clearance	0.020~0.057 (0.024~0.061)	0.15 (0.15)
Journal	Shaft outside diameter	$\phi 40 \begin{smallmatrix}0\\-0.015\end{smallmatrix}$ ($\phi 50 \begin{smallmatrix}0\\-0.015\end{smallmatrix}$)	39.90 (49.90)
	Bearing inside diameter	$\phi 40 \begin{smallmatrix}+0.038\\+0.010\end{smallmatrix}$ ($\phi 50 \begin{smallmatrix}+0.041\\+0.010\end{smallmatrix}$)	40.08 (50.08)
	Oil clearance	0.010~0.053 (0.010~0.056)	0.15 (0.15)

( ) for D36A

Chapter 3 Inspection and Service Procedures for Engine Parts
5. Camshaft
SM/D27A & D36A

5. Camshaft

The intake/exhaust cams, the fuel cam and the journals of the camshaft are surface hardened and grounded. The camshaft drives the lube oil pump, linked at its end.

1. Points for reassembling and servicing

   (1) Measuring outside diameter of camshaft and inside diameter of journal
   Measure the camshaft. If it is damaged excessively, replace it.

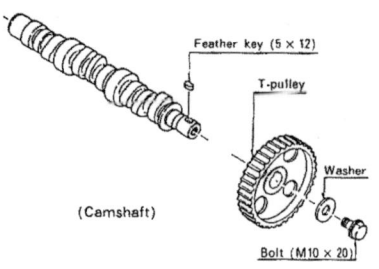
(Camshaft)

(mm)

	Standard	Wear limit
Camshaft outside diameter	$\phi 41 \begin{smallmatrix} -0.050 \\ -0.075 \end{smallmatrix}$ ($\phi 49 \begin{smallmatrix} -0.050 \\ -0.075 \end{smallmatrix}$)	40.9 (48.9)
Camshaft journal inside diameter	$\phi 41 \begin{smallmatrix} +0.025 \\ 0 \end{smallmatrix}$ ($\phi 49 \begin{smallmatrix} +0.025 \\ 0 \end{smallmatrix}$)	41.07 (49.07)
Oil clearance	0.050~0.100 (0.050~0.100)	0.15 (0.15)

( ) for D36A

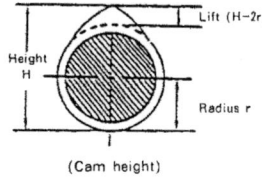
(Cam height)

(Cam height)

(mm)

	Standard	Wear limit
Intake cam height (H)	34.965 (41.928)	−0.1 (−0.1)
Exhaust cam height (H)	34.965 (41.928)	−0.1 (−0.1)
Fuel cam height (H)	33.436 (42.943)	−0.1 (−0.1)

( ) for D36A

6. Cylinder head

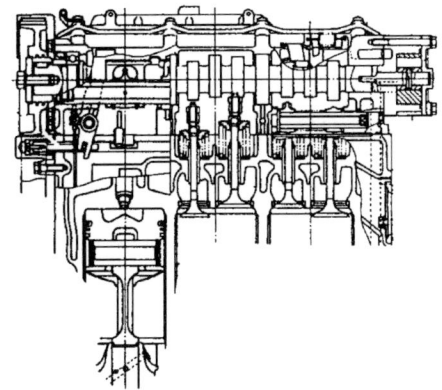

- The integrated cylinder head for the 3 cylinders is built in the cylinder block.
- Each cylinder has intake and exhaust valves, both fitted with the valve seat insert.

1. Cautions when reassembling and servicing

   (1) Inspection of combustion surface for cracks
   The combustion surface is used under severe conditions, including exposure to the extreme high temperature and pressure and also the low temperature of the intake air. Check the combustion surface for discolorations, distortions and cracks with a color checker.

   (2) Inspection of intake/exhaust valve seat
   Check the intake/exhaust valve seat for the contact condition and the width. If the seat surface width exceeds the wear limit or the surface is too coarse, modify the seat.

   (3) Procedures for grinding intake/exhaust valve seat
   Do the following procedures to modify the intake/exhaust valve seat with a seat grinder.

   1) Seat specification

Intake valve seat	Angle : 45°
Exhaust valve seat	Angle : 45°

   Standard interference
   (mm)

	D27A	D36A
Intake valve seat	0.058~0.094	0.088~0.124
Exhaust valve seat	0.050~0.083	0.067~0.103

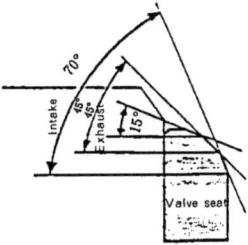

(Modifying intake/exhaust valve seat)

   2) Be sure to measure the clearance between the valve and the valve guide, if modifications are needed. If the clearance exceeds the wear limit, replace the valve or the valve guide before grinding.
   3) Knead valve compound with oil, and grind the valve seat with the compound.
   4) Grind the valve seat with oil only.
   5) After grinding the valve seat, wash the valve and the cylinder head with diesel fuel oil carefully so that the valve compound or the grounded powder does not remains.

Chapter 3 Inspection and Service Procedures for Engine Parts
6. Cylinder Head

(4) Inspection of intake/exhaust valve and valve guide

- The cylinder head has one intake valve and one exhaust valve (two-valve system). The O.H.C. system driven by the timing belt is employed for the valve driving.
- The intake and exhaust valves are mushroom-shaped with a valve head cap.

1) Inspection of valve stem for wear and distortion
   Check the valve stem for wear and distortion. If the valve stem is distorted or exceeds the wear limit, replace it. (Also replace the valve guide at the same time.)

(mm)

		Standard	Wear limit
Valve stem outside diameter	Intake	φ7 $_{-0.045}^{-0.030}$	6.92
	Exhaust	φ7 $_{-0.045}^{-0.030}$	6.92

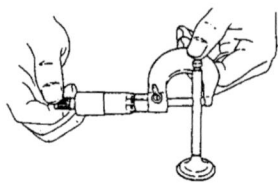
(Measuring valve stem)

2) Inspection of valve recess
   After the valve has been repeatedly grounded, the valve recesses. Excessive valve recess affects the combustion performance. Accordingly, measure the recess, and if it exceeds the wear limit, replace the valve and the seat.

(mm)

Valve recess		Standard	Wear limit
D27A	Intake	0.25±0.1	0.5
	Exhaust	⊖0.50±0.1	⊖0.25
D36A	Intake	0.25±0.1	0.5
	Exhaust	0.45±0.1	0.7

⊖is the projecting size

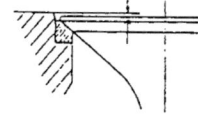
(Intake/exhaust valve recess)

3) Measuring the valve guide inside diameter
   Measure the inside diameter of the valve guide. Replace it, if it exceeds the wear limit.

Chapter 3 Inspection and Service Procedures for Engine Parts
6. Cylinder Head

SM/D27A & D36A

4) Inspection of intake/exhaust valve spring
- Check the intake/exhaust valve spring for flaws and corrosion. Replace the valve spring, if there are any flaws or corrosion.
- Measure the free length of the spring.
- Measure the tension of the spring. (Use a spring tension meter, if available.)
- Measure the slant of the spring (the angle of the side of the spring).

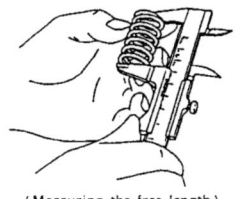

(mm)

		Standard	Wear limit
Valve spring	Free length (Outer/Inner)	37.4 (43/40.7)	36 (41.5/39)
	Compressive force (kgf) (1mm Compressive force)	2.37 1.87	—
	Slant	1.6	2.0

( ) for D36A

NOTE: The more dense spring painted is installed to the cylinder block side.

(Measuring the free length of the spring)

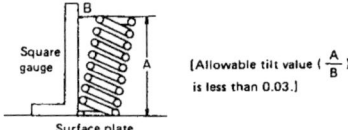

[Allowable tilt value ($\frac{A}{B}$) is less than 0.03.]

(5) Replacing the valve seat
- The valve seat is cold-fitted to the cylinder block. Accordingly, welding is suitable for removing a valve seat.
- As shown in the right diagram, weld the seat removing rod (an exhaust valve is attached later) to the weld-removing piece at three parts, and knock the rod to remove the seat.
- Be sure to clamp the ⊖ side of the welder to the seat removing rod (shown in the diagram) when welding.
- Protect the spudder on the explosion surface of the cylinder with teflon seats. (Refer to the SERVICE NEWS 92MB-006.) Press-fit the valve seat with a guide and a hammer (special tools).

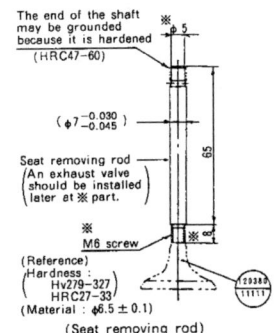

(Seat removing rod)

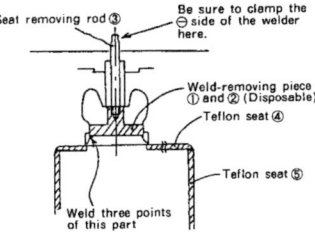

(Seat removing method)

Printed in Japan
A0A5055-JC03

3-11

Chapter 3 Inspection and Service Procedures for Engine Parts
6. Cylinder Head

(6) Replacing the valve guide
- Remove the valve guide from the inside of the cylinder to the valve arm case side. (The cylinder might be scratched by the peripheral grooves on the valve guide if removed to the opposite side of the valve arm case.
- Take care not to damage the clip on the intake port when removing the valve guide.
- Press-fit the valve guide with a positioning piece and a press-fitting tool.
- Finish the inside diameter of the valve guide with a hand reamer (120270-99780) after press-fitting.

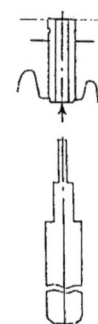
(Removing tool 120270-99770)

	ϕ D	L
D27A	$25^{\pm 0.1}$	$45^{\pm 0.1}$
D36A	$30^{\pm 30}$	$47.5^{\pm 0.1}$

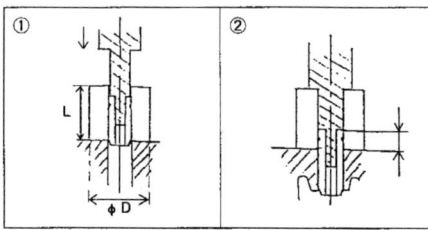
(Positioning the valve guide)

(mm)

	Standard	Wear limit
Inside diameter of intake/exhaust valve guide	$\phi 7 \; ^{+0.020}_{+0.005}$	7.08
Clearance between intake/exhaust valve and valve guide	0.035~0.065	0.12

NOTE: A valve stem seal is attached on the intake/exhaust valve guides. Replace the valve stem seal with new one if removed once, because it is not reusable. As for D36A, the valve stem seals for the intake valve and the exhaust valve differ from each other in shape, so be careful of the type of the valve stem seal. Use the press-fitting tool described in p. 2-3.

(Hand reamer)

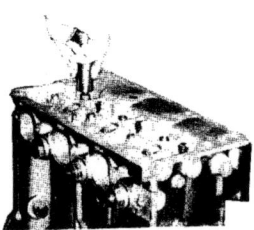
(Install the valve stem seal (Special tool))

7. Valve Arm Case

The valve arm case houses the intake/exhaust valve arm shaft, fuel valve arm shaft, camshaft, decompression device and breather.

1. Cautions for reassembling and servicing

    (1) Measuring the inside diameter of camshaft journal in valve arm case
    Measure the camshaft journal inside diameter. Replace the camshaft journal, if worn beyond the limit.

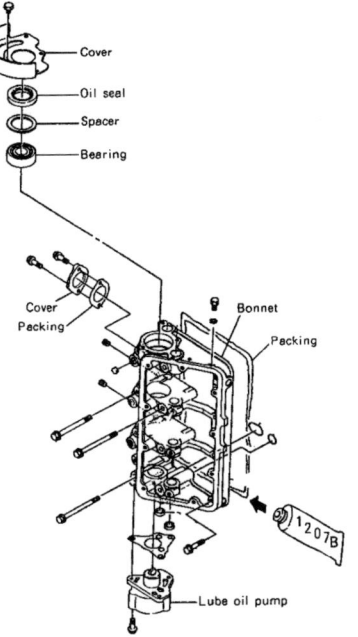

(mm)

	Standard		Wear limit
Bearing (6006) inside diameter	φ47 (φ55)	−0.030 −0.050	46.99 (54.99)
Mid-journal inside diameter	φ41 (φ49)	+0.025 0	41.07 (49.07)
L0 pump side journal inside diameter	φ26	+0.021 0	26.05

( ) for D36A

(2) Use new packings, oil seals and O-ring.
(3) Do not remove the plugs or the blind caps except when necessary.
(4) Clean the camshaft journal, bearing (6006) and valve arm shaft journal carefully before installing.

(Valve arm case)

8. Intake/Exhaust Valve Arm and Unit Injector

- The intake/exhaust valve arms are rocker-lever type.
- The unit injector driving valve arm is rocker arm type, and the roller type is used for the cam contact side.

1. Cautions for reassembling and servicing

   (1) Measuring outside diameter of intake/exhaust valve arm shaft and inside diameter of intake/exhaust valve arm

   Measure the outside diameter of the intake/exhaust valve arm shaft and the inside diameter of the valve arm. Replace the intake/exhaust valve arm shaft or the valve arm, if worn beyond the limit.

   (mm)

	Standard	Wear limit
Intake/exhaust valve arm shaft outside diameter	$\phi 16\,^{-0.016}_{-0.034}$	15.90
Intake/exhaust valve arm inside diameter	$\phi 16\,^{+0.018}_{0}$ ($\phi 16\,^{+0.006}_{-0.012}$)	16.03
Clearance between valve arm shaft outside diameter and valve arm inside diameter	0.016~0.052 (0.004~0.040)	0.13

   ( ) for D36A

   (2) Measuring outside diameter of injector driving valve arm shaft and inside diameter of valve arm

   - Measure the outside diameter of the injector driving valve arm shaft and the inside diameter of the valve arm. Replace the injector driving valve arm shaft or the valve arm, if worn beyond the limit.

   (mm)

	Standard	Wear limit
Unit injector driving valve arm shaft outside diameter	$\phi 16\,^{-0.016}_{-0.034}$ ($\phi 22\,^{-0.020}_{-0.041}$)	15.88 (21.88)
Unit injector driving valve arm inside diameter	$\phi 16\,^{+0.018}_{0}$ ($\phi 22\,^{+0.021}_{0}$)	16.03 (22.03)
Clearance between valve arm shaft outside diameter and valve arm inside diameter	0.016~0.052 (0.004~0.040)	0.15

   ( ) for D36A

   - Inspection of injector driving valve arm roller
   Check the roller pins on the injector driving valve arm. If flaws, cracks, or wear is excessive, replace the pin.

   (mm)

	Nominal	Wear limit
Roller pin outside diameter	$\phi 7$	6.96

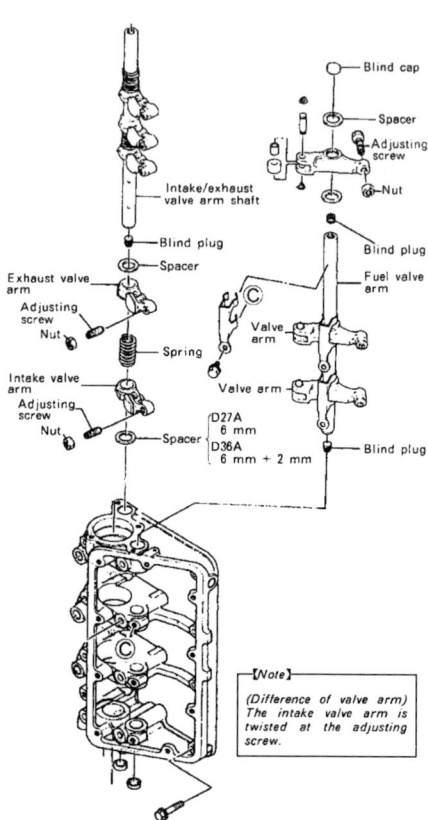

-[Note]-

(Difference of valve arm) The intake valve arm is twisted at the adjusting screw.

(3) Measuring top clearance

Measuring procedure

a. Remove the unit injector.
b. Turn the flywheel to position the piston at approximately 20° before the top dead center.
c. Insert the measuring fuse (1.0mm diameter) through the unit injector installation hole, and place the fuse at the position illustrated on the right. (The space is too small to accept more than one fuse.)
d. Turn the flywheel in the regular turning direction (clockwise viewed from the flywheel side) to position at approximately 20° after the top dead center, and take out the measuring fuse.
e. Measure the thickness of the pressed measuring fuse with a micrometer.

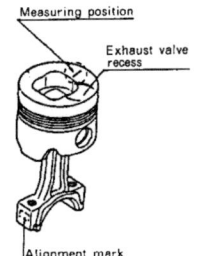

Measuring position
Exhaust valve recess

Alignment mark

(mm)

		Standard
Top clearance	D27A	$0.60^{\pm 0.05}$
	D36A	$0.55^{\pm 0.05}$

(4) Adjusting valve clearance of intake/exhaust valve head

Adjusting procedure

Take out the unit injector valve arm retainer.

a. Adjust the clearance while the engine is cool.
b. Position the piston at the top dead center of the combustion stroke. (Top compression)
c. Loosen the adjusting screws and nuts of the intake/exhaust valve arms.
d. Adjust the clearances between the intake/exhaust valve heads and adjusting screw heads to the specified value, lock the adjusting screws.

NOTE: 1. Make sure that the caps are installed to the intake/exhaust valve heads before adjusting.
2. Refer to p. 3-29 if the timing gear pulley is disassembled.

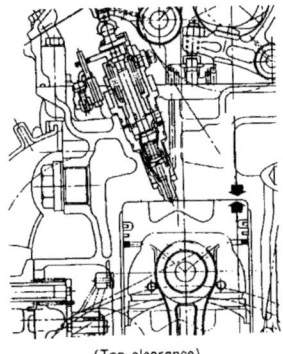

(Top clearance)

(mm)

		Standard
Intake/exhaust valve head clearance	Intake	0.2
	Exhaust	0.2

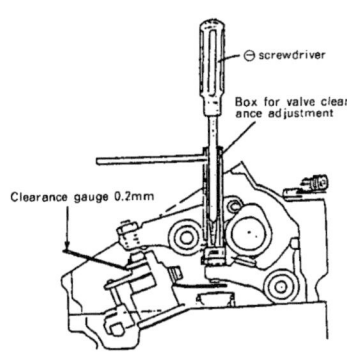

⊖ screwdriver

Box for valve clearance adjustment

Clearance gauge 0.2mm

(Intake/exhaust valve head clearance adjustment)

Chapter 3 Inspection and Service Procedures for Engine Parts
8. Intake/Exhaust Valve Arm and Unit Injector

(5) Adjusting fuel injection timing
Adjusting when the unit injector is installed on the engine
Install the unit injector on the engine. Align the scale of the flywheel to the specified injection timing. Turn the adjusting screw until the tappet line matches up the alignment line on the injector body viewed from A (illustrated on the right diagram). Fix the adjusting screw with lock nuts.

NOTE: For adjustment use a deflection mirror.

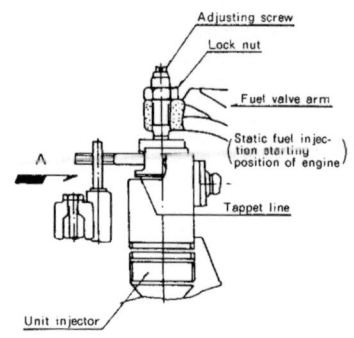

(Adjusting fuel injection timing)

	Standard	
	D36A	D27A
Fuel injection timing (FIC)	bTDC 15°	bTDC 12°

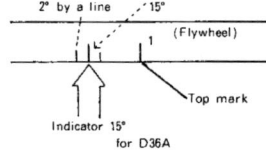

Indicator 15° for D36A

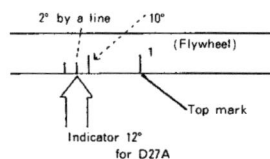

Indicator 12° for D27A

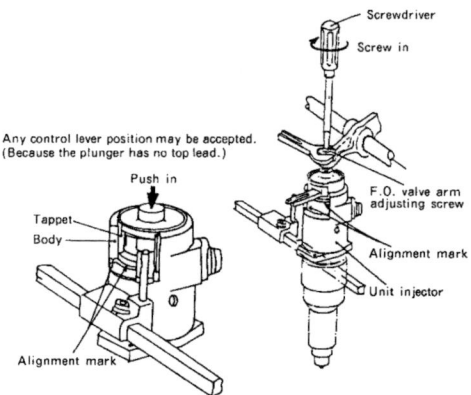

3-16

Printed in Japan
A0A5055-JC03

9. Thermostat

Two wax-pellet type thermostats of the same shape are installed to the cylinder block side cover, one for the water temperature and one for the exhaust temperature. These thermostats keep the temperature according to the water temperature and the load.

1. Cautions for reassembling and servicing

    (1) Inspection of thermostat

    a. Place the thermostat in a container filled with water. Measure the water temperature with a thermometer while heating the water. If the valve opens at the specified valve opening temp. and opens fully at the specified valve full-open temp., the thermostat is good. If the valve opening or full-open temperature of the thermostat differs from the specified temp., replace the thermostat.

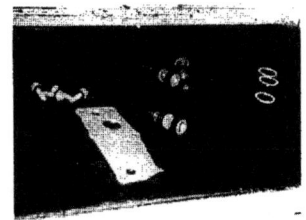

(Jiggle valve, thermostat cover and thermostat)

	Standard temperature ℃		YANMAR code No.
	Valve opening temp.	Valve full-open temp.	
Water temp. thermostat	72℃	82℃	120270-49191
Exhaust temp. thermostat	65℃	75℃	120270-49203

b. Use new packings and seal washers.
c. Tighten the bolts (M6 X 25, M6 X 50) at the specified torque.

Bolt (M6×25, M6×50) Tightening torque	Width (10) 0.8~1.0 kgf-m

d. Remove any dust from the thermostat.

(Install the thermostat)

Chapter 3 Inspection and Service Procedures for Engine Parts
10. Unit Injector_____SM/D27A & D36A

10. Unit Injector

The unit injector is an integral part of the fuel injection pump and the nozzle, and is installed to each cylinder.
- Pump : Bosch type control system (by control lever)
- Nozzle : Sealed automatic valve, wheel valve

1. Specifications

Pump type		M-type unit injector	
		D36A	D27A
Plunger diameter	mm	$\phi 7$	$\phi 6$
Nozzle injection hole	mm	$5 - \phi 0.22 \times 155°$	$4 - \phi 0.20 \times 150°$
Pre-stroke	mm	3.0	2.5
Cam lift	mm	7.0	6.5
Fuel valve opening pressure	kgf/cm²	$200^{\pm 5}$	←

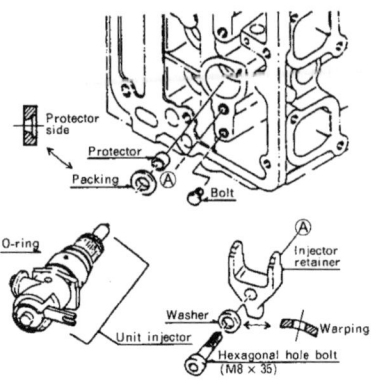

(Unit injector)

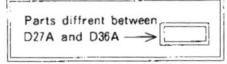

Parts diffrent between D27A and D36A →

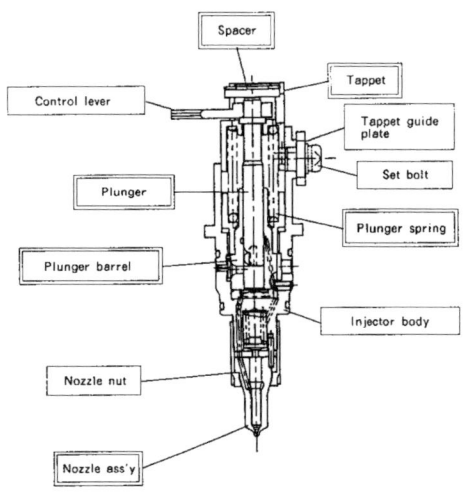

(Unit injector assembly)

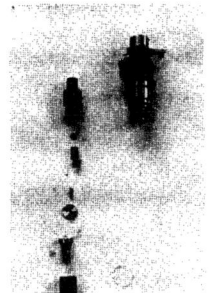

(Nozzle adjusting holder and nozzle)

3-18

Printed in Japan
A0A5055-JC03

Chapter 3 Inspection and Service Procedures for Engine Parts
10. Unit Injector
SM/D27A & D36A

2. Disassembling the unit injector
   Disassemble and adjust the unit injector body at a service shop.
   Follow the procedures below to check the opening valve pressure adjustment and the spray form of the nozzle.

   (1) Inspection of nozzle assembly

   a. Carbon flower
   A phenomenon that carbon sticks to the nozzle like a flower is called carbon flower. As carbon flower reduces combustion performance, remove the carbon if any.

   b. Spray shape
   1) Check the spray with a nozzle tester.
   2) Normal spray shape (illustrated below)

   - No excessive angle deviation.
   - The spray is fine mist.
   - The spray stops instantaneously.

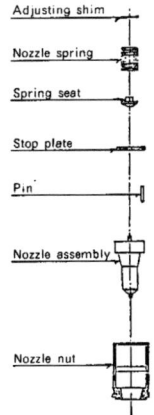

(Nozzle disassembly)

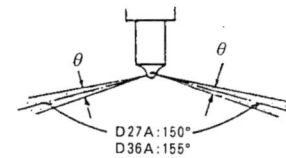

D27A : 150°
D36A : 155°

(Normal spray shape)

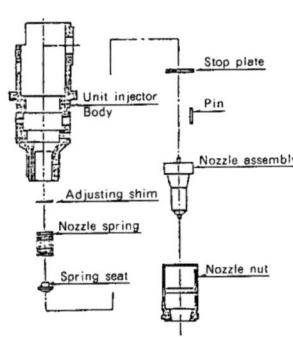

(Disassembling the nozzle assembly)

(2) Adjusting nozzle valve opening pressure
   1) Remove the nozzle from the unit injector.
   2) Install the nozzle to the adjusting holder.
      Assemble the adjusting shim, nozzle spring, spring seat and stop plate, and install the assembly.

Tightening torque	4.0~4.5 kgf-m

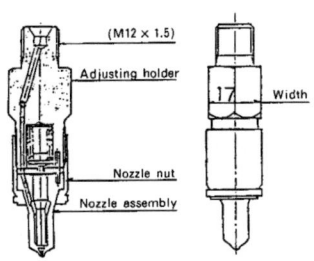

(Adjusting holder assembly)

Chapter 3 Inspection and Service Procedures for Engine Parts
10. Unit Injector
SM/D27A & D36A

3) Test with a nozzle tester.

Valve opening pressure	$200^{\pm 5}$ kgf-cm²

NOTE: If the nozzle assembly has been used less than 500 hours, the pressure is hardly changed by replacing the nozzle assembly.

4) Adjust the nozzle valve opening pressure.
Measure the depths of the inserted parts of the unit injector body and the spring bracket. Adjust the pressure by increasing or reducing the thickness of the adjusting shim.
Compare the depths of H and H₁ illustrated on the right diagram, and adjust the thickness of the adjusting shim (described below).

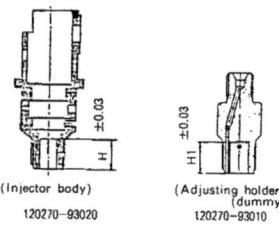

(Nozzle tester)

ID	Shim thickness
25	0.25
30	0.30
35	0.35
40	0.40
45	0.45
50	0.50
55	0.55

─[NOTE]─
1. The ID. is displayed with permanent ink.

   | 45 |

2. 0.1mm adjusting shim increases or reduces 20 kgf/cm² valve opening pressure.
3. Use one adjusting shim. (2 or more adjusting shim are forbidden.)

(Injector body)
120270-93020

(Adjusting holder) (dummy)
120270-93010

Standard size
H=H1=13.9mm

Valve opening pressure adjusting holder 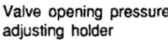 120270-93010

[Confirmations]

Confirm the following before installing to the unit injector body:

Install the nozzle adjusted at 200 ± 5kgf/cm² with the adjusting holder, spring and shim to the unit injector. Tighten the case nuts after readjusting H₁ and H.

Example:

(1) Dimension of shim adjusted at 200 ± 5kgf/cm²
    (shim thickness of nozzle valve opening pressure adjusting holder)   0.45
(2) Dimension of H (depth of injector body nozzle spring case)   13.95
(3) Dimension of H₁ (depth of nozzle valve opening pressure adjusting holder nozzle spring case)   13.90
    0.45 + (13.95 − 3.90) = 0.50   (thickness of shim in unit injector assembly)

NOTE: Replace the packing, protector and O-ring with new ones when installing the unit injector to the engine.

Chapter 3 Inspection and Service Procedures for Engine Parts
10. Unit Injector

(Procedures for adjusting nozzle valve opening pressure)

(1) Install the unit injector holder to the vise base.

(2) Set the unit injector to the holder.

(3) Loosen the case nuts, and remove the nozzle from the unit injector.

(4) Install the nozzle to the adjusting holder.

(5) Install the adjusting holder to the nozzle tester, and adjust the valve opening pressure with the adjusting shim.

Chapter 3 Inspection and Service Procedures for Engine Parts
10. Unit Injector
SM/D27A & D36A

3. Removing unit injector

   (1) Be sure to remove fuel oil or to tilt up the engine before removing the unit injector (to prevent fuel leak at the fuel pass).
   (2) Align to the overlap position.
   (3) Loosen the injector fixing bolt, and remove the retainer. (6-mm hexagon rod wrench)
   (4) Down the FO valve arm.
   (5) Screw a fixing bolt, and lever the cut of the injector up with removing tool using the bolt as a supporter.

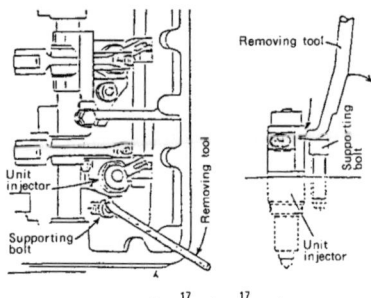

4. Standards for servicing (unit injector)

   (1) Reference of standards for servicing

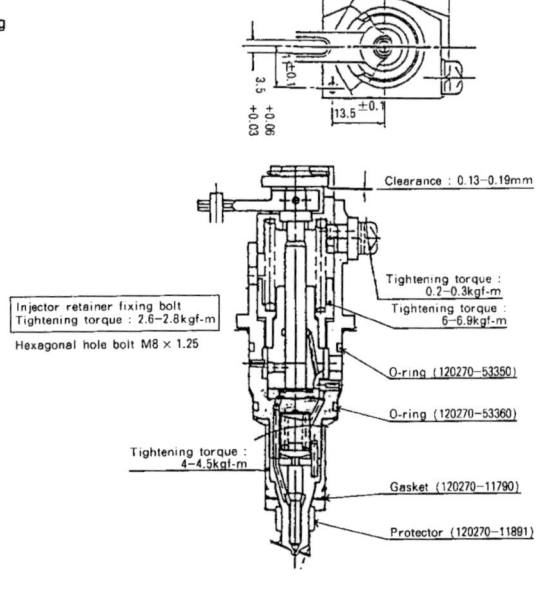

   (2) Adjusting tools

No.	Name	Q'ty	Remark	No.	Name	Q'ty	Remark
1	Nozzle tester	1	727610-93100 (including high pressure pipe)	6	Slide caliper	1	Commercial tool
2	High pressure pipe	1	127610-93400 (High pressure pipe)	7	Unit injector holder	1	120270-93020
3	Torque wrench (900QL)	1	Commercial tool	8	Nozzle valve opening pressure adjusting holder	1	120270-93010
4	Box wrench 15 mm	1	Commercial tool (12 pieces)	9	Vise base	1	Commercial tool
5	Spanner 17 × 19	2	Commercial tool	10			

Chapter 3 Inspection and Service Procedures for Engine Parts
10. Unit Injector
SM/D27A & D36A

5. Fuel feed pump

(1) Specifications

r.p.m.	3900rpm
Feeding quantity	1.3 ℓ/min or more
Feeding pressure	1.0kgf/cm² or more
Oil temperature	60 ± 5 °C
Efficiency	80%
r.p.m.	780rpm
Feeding quantity	0.09 ℓ/min or more
Feeding pressure	0.7kgf/cm² or more
Intake head	-500mm
Resisting pressure	2.0kgf/cm²
Oil	Diesel fuel oil

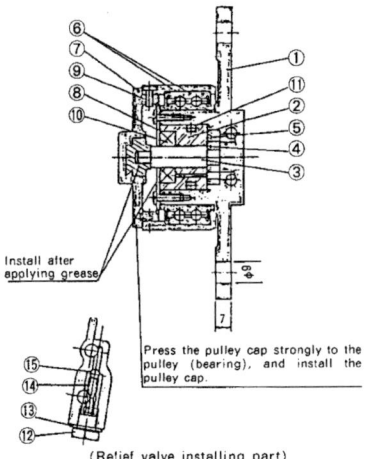

Install after applying grease

Press the pulley cap strongly to the pulley (bearing), and install the pulley cap.

(Relief valve installing part)

(2) Composition

	Parts	Code No.	Q'ty
1	Body	120270-52302	1
2	Cover (FOP)	〃 52310	1
3	Shaft (FOP)	〃 52320	1
4	Inner rotor	〃 52330	1
5	Outer rotor	〃 52340	1
6	Pulley (Bearing)	〃 52800	1
7	Pulley (cap)	〃 52811	1
8	Plate	〃 52121	1
9	Binding small screw (M3 × 7)	〃 52820	10
10	Oil seal	〃 52140	1
11	O-ring	24311-350220	1
12	Hexagon plug	23887-080002	1
13	Seal washer	43400-500410	1
14	Spring	120270-52390	1
15	Steel ball (3/16)	24190-060001	1

(3) Cautions when reassembling
- The bearing pulley ⑥ must turn smoothly.
- The O-ring ⑪ must be applied with silicon oil.
- The binding small screws (M3) ⑨ must be plated screws.
  (120270-52820-RM)

Chapter 3 Inspection and Service Procedures for Engine Parts
11. Governor _____ *SM/D27A & D36A*

11. Governor

The governor is a 3-point weight mechanical all-speed governor. Also this is a floating lever type governor driven by the timing belt, and installed to the cylinder block.
The governor weight assembly is driven by the timing belt pulley and controls the unit injector control rod via the governor lever to control (increase/decrease) fuel injection volume.

1. Cautions when reassembling and servicing

   (1) Inspection of governor
   To protect the engine, the governor is adjusted to the specified output and engine speed, and sealed and locked with fixing wire. Accordingly, do not disassemble and adjust the governor unless necessary. Improper adjusting of the governor causes engine troubles or operation failures.

   (Governor assembly)

   (2) When the governor is disassembled, check the following:

   a. Governor weight pin
   Measure the outside and the inside diameter of the governor weight pin. Replace the governor weight pin, if it is worn.

   (mm)

	Standard	Wear limit
Governor weight pin outside diameter	$\phi 6 \; {}^{+0.012}_{+0.004}$	5.99
Governor weight pin hole inside diameter	$\phi 6 \; {}^{+0.10}_{+0.05}$	6.15

   b. Thrust needle
   Check the thrust needle for seizure, discoloration or damage. Replace any defective thrust needle.

   c. Governor spindle and governor weight support
   Check the outside of the governor spindle and the inside of the governor weight support for seizure, discoloration or damage. Replace any defective governor spindle or governor weight support.

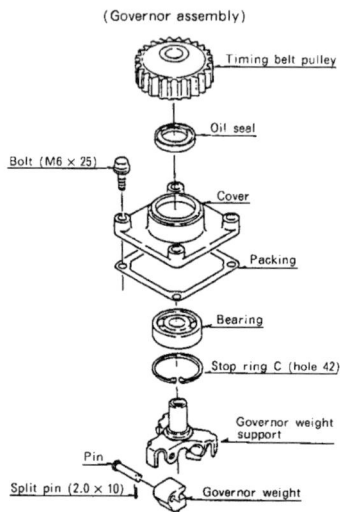

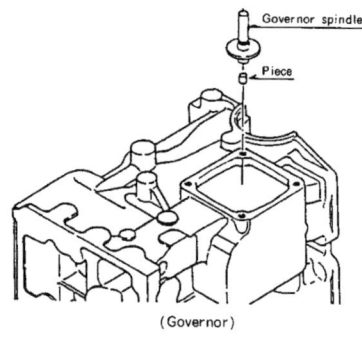

(Governor)

Chapter 3 Inspection and Service Procedures for Engine Parts
11. Governor
SM/D27A & D36A

2. Adjusting procedures when reassembling
   (1) Adjusting unit injector injection volume on each cylinder
      1) Press and fix the control rod against the end surface of the cover (start SP) with a fixing jig.

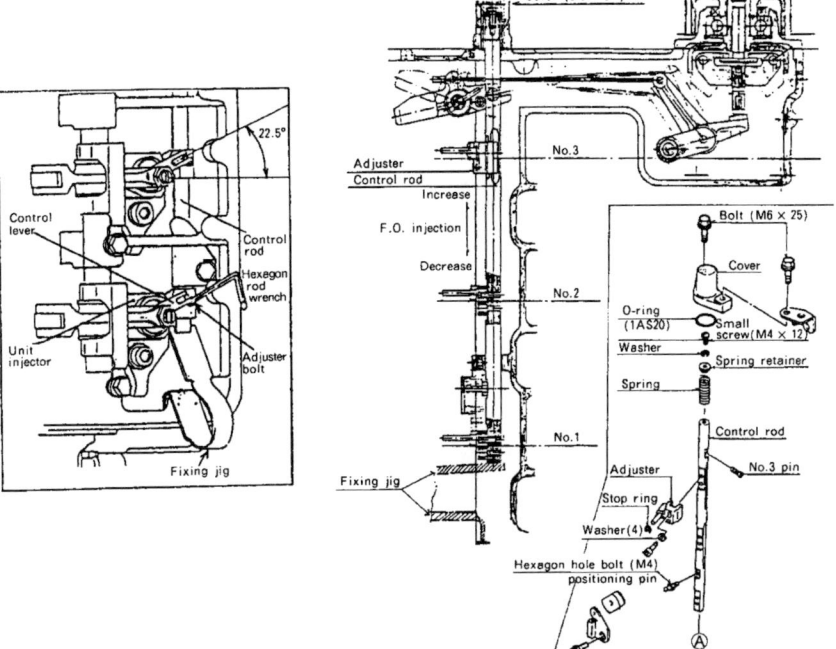

2) Turn each of the unit injector control levers to the fuel increasing side. Fix the adjuster to the control rod with a hexagon hole bolt and a washer, while pressing the lever against the side of the tappet.

NOTE: Check the control lever for any play by moving the lever. Readjust the control lever, if necessary. The clearance must be 0 for all three control levers.

Hexagon hole bolt (M4 × 18) tightening torque	0.08~0.11 kgf-m

Chapter 3 Inspection and Service Procedures for Engine Parts
11. Governor
SM/D27A & D36A

3) Remove the fixing jig, and make sure that the control rod moves smoothly.

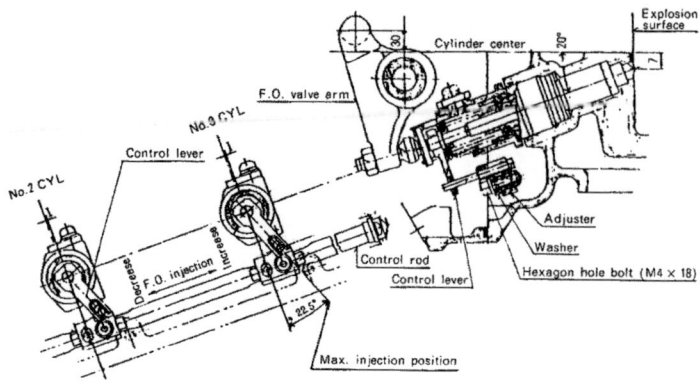

(2) Adjusting regulator spring assembly

1) The fitting load of the regulator spring is already adjusted at our plant. Do not remove the assembly. When the no load speed cannot be raised to more than 4800 rpm, add the adjusting shim to adjust the speed.

2) Check the installation length of the idle spring. Make sure that the stroke is 4 ±0.3 mm after setting the idle adjuster to the dimension ℓ (ℓ = 6 mm).

3) Set the spring (A) at its free length to the idle spring retainer. Make sure that the stroke of the spring (A) is 2 ± 0.3 mm, before reassembling it to the regulator spring case.

(3) Adjusting the governor

1) Max. speed
Screw in the regulator spring case manually until it contacts the governor lever 1. (This position is at the medium speed spring, not where it is fully screwed in with a wrench.) Then, unscrew the case by 2.5 turns (5 mm). The max. speed 4800 − 4900 rpm should be obtained at this position. If the max. speed can not be obtained, screw the case in further.

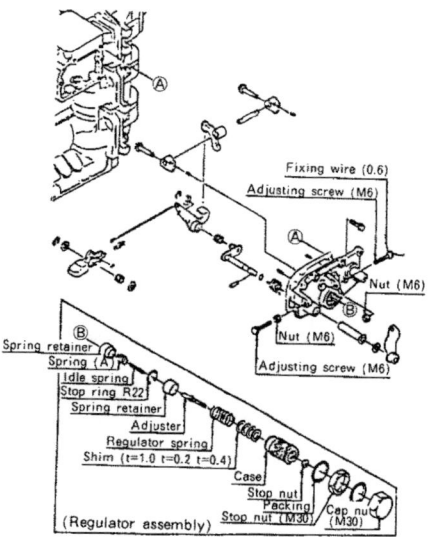

Printed in Japan
A0A5055-IC03

Chapter 3 Inspection and Service Procedures for Engine Parts
11. Governor

SM/D27A & D36A

2) Min. speed
   Protrude the idling adjuster 6.0 mm from the case end.

- Idling fine adjustment : Make fine adjustment with the idle adjusting bolt, and set the speed to 1000 rpm.
- Max. load adjustment : Adjust to 4500 rpm with the fuel regulating bolt during cruising or by installing the load equipment.

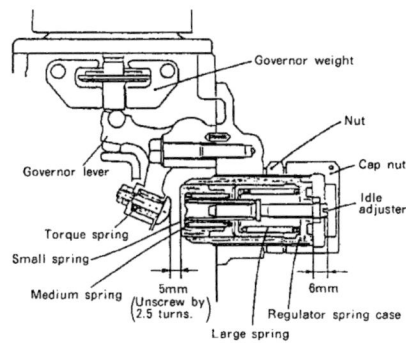

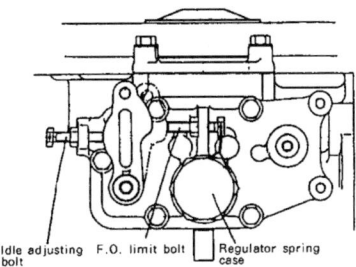

(4) Adjusting governor link

1) Adjusting regulator cable
   Turn the steering handle grip in the increasing direction, and fix the grip at where it contacts the stopper. Adjust the regulator cable so that the alignment marks match up. (About 25° from the vertical line level.)

2) Adjusting regulator rod length

   a) Turn the steering handle grip in the increasing direction, and fix the grip at where it contacts the stopper.
   b) Screw in the rod spring stop nut until the regulator lever reaches the max. position (where the nut contacts the limit bolt).
   c) Further screw in the stop nut by 2 turns (about 2 mm), and fix the nut.

3) Adjusting reverse rod length
   Turn the steering handle grip to the max. speed position. Adjust the clearance between the reverse lever stopper and the bracket (shift) to approximately 2 mm at the max. speed position.

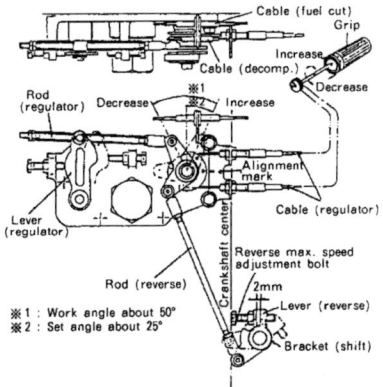

※1 : Work angle about 50°
※2 : Set angle about 25°

Chapter 3 Inspection and Service Procedures for Engine Parts
11. Governor _____ *SM/D27A & D36A*

(5) Adjusting engine speed
Adjust the idling and the max. speed to the specified load applied to the propeller shaft of the outboard engine.

1) Adjusting the idling speed (1000 rpm when the engine is warm)
Shift the clutch to the neutral position. Adjust the idling speed with the idle adjusting bolt so that the engine speed is in the range of 1000 ~1050 rpm, and lock the bolt with nut.

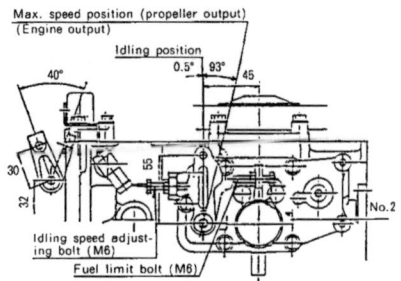

Nut (M6) tightening torque	Width ⑩ 0.8~1.0kgf-m

2) Adjusting max. speed (4600 rpm)

- Shift the clutch to the forward position. Adjust the max. speed with the fuel limit bolt so that the engine speed is in the range of 4400 ~ 4600 rpm, and lock the bolt with a nut.

Nut (M6) tightening torque	Width ⑩ 0.8~1.0kgf-m

- Fasten the nut to the fuel limit bolt cap nut with a fixing wire (⌀0.6 mm), and seal it.

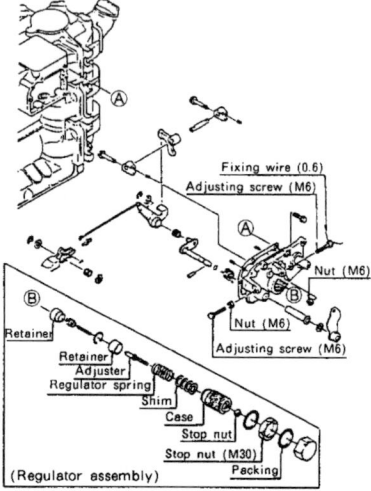

3-28

Chapter 3 Inspection and Service Procedures for Engine Parts
11. Governor

(6) Procedures for installing timing belt

1) Removing the timing belt
   a) Install the fixture to the flywheel, and loosen the flywheel fixing bolts.
   b) Remove the flywheel with a flywheel removing tool.
   c) Remove the generator, loosen the belt tensioner of the feed pump, and remove the timing belt.

NOTE: To remove the timing belt, align the marks as shown in the illustration.

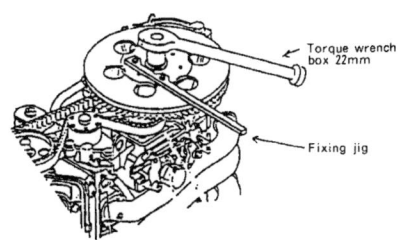

2) Installing the timing belt

   a) Align the crank gear alignment mark with the cam pulley alignment mark, and set the belt.
   b) Tighten the feed pump tensioner.

   Belt tension
   • New belt   : Adjust the tension to 15kg with a belt tension gauge.
   • Reused belt : Measure the tension with a belt tension gauge before removing the belt, and adjust the tension to the measurement after installing the belt. Or mark on the tensioner and the cylinder before removing the belt, and adjust the tension by aligning the marks after installing the belt.

   (Do not clean the belt with grease or oil.)

   c) Install the generator.
      (Apply screw lock to the installation bolts.)
   d) Install the flywheel.

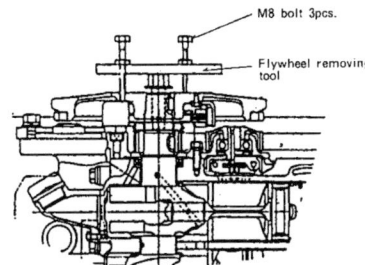

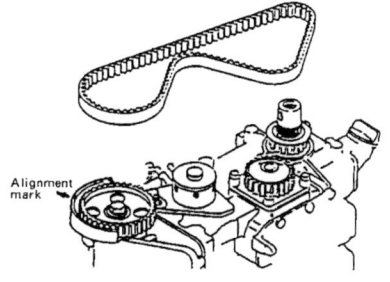

Box wrench 36mm	28kgf-m

Model	Belt code	Size
D36A	120380-01430	111R25 (Belt width 25)
D27A	120270-01430	101R19 (Belt width 19)

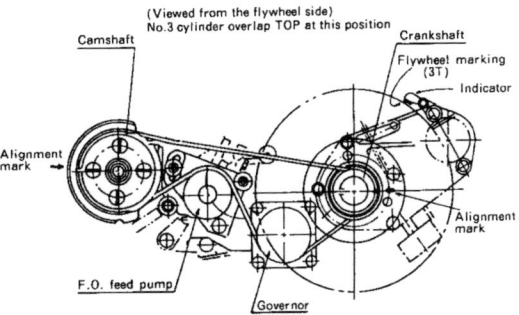

CHAPTER 4

REASSEMBLING AND SERVICING OF DRIVE UNIT

1. Swivel/Steering Bracket 4-1
2. Clamp Bracket 4-4
3. Upper Case 4-5
4. Bottom Cowling and Fitting Parts 4-6
5. Lower Gear Case 4-9
6. Cooling Water Pump and Cooling Water Piping 4-15
7. Steering Handle 4-16
8. Hydraulic Cylinder 4-17
9. Electric-Hydraulic Tilting 4-18
10. Connecting the Upper Case with Steering Bracket 4-20

Chapter 4 Reassembling and Servicing of Drive Unit
1. Swivel/Steering Bracket

1. Swivel/Steering Bracket

The swivel bracket is connected to the clamp bracket with the tilt tube, and supports the steering bracket with the pivot shaft. The pivot shaft bearing is sealed and is equipped with the brake. The steering bracket is separate from the handle bracket or the lower mount bracket, and is connected by a spline and a stop ring.

1. Cautions when reassembling and servicing

    (1) The steering bracket is separate from the pivot shaft.
    (2) Swivel bracket
    - a. Install the friction plate, bush (45 X 30), O-ring and washer in that order to the upper part of the pivot shaft hole of the swivel bracket.
    - b. Install the pivot shaft to the pivot shaft hole of the swivel bracket.
    - c. Install the bush (30 X 44), seal (VC30405) and washer in that order to the lower part of the pivot shaft hole of the swivel bracket.

(Install the upper bush)

	Standard
Clearance between bush inside dia. and outside dia.	0~1.1mm

- d. Install the lower mount bracket and a washer stop ring.

(Swivel bracket)

(Lower mount)

Chapter 4 Reassembling and Servicing of Drive Unit
1. Swivel/Steering Bracket

SM/D27A & D36A

e. Tilt lock lever
   The reassembling procedures and the parts are not the same for manual tilting and the hydraulic tilting. (Refer to p. 4-18.)

   Cautions when reassembling each parts are described here.

   1) Fit in the left and right tilt lock levers.

	Standard
Clearance between tilt lock lever shaft outside dia. and bearing inside dia.	0.06~0.174mm

(Knock in the sleeve bearing)

   Set washers, return spring, collars, tilt spring hooks, and tilt stop levers to the both ends of the tilt lock levers (L and R). Match up the hole of the tilt lock levers (L and R) and the collars, and fix them with split pins (3.2 X 2.5). Before fixing, hang the return springs on the tilt spring hooks.

   2) Fasten the tilt lever bolt to the return spring and the tilt spring hook, and set the assembly to the tilt lock levers.

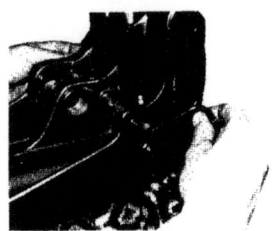
(Install the tilt lock levers)

NOTE: 1. Supply grease to the pivot shaft, tilt lock lever shaft and the tilt lever bearing parts.

   Recommended grease :
      COSMO GREASE DYNAMAX EP No.2
      or equivalent

   2. Install the bush (30 X 39) to the swivel bracket in advance.

	Standard
Clearance between bush outside dia. and bracket hole inside dia.	0~0.25mm

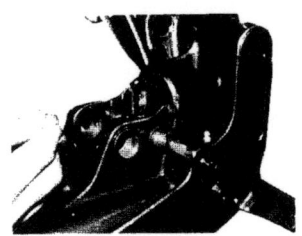
(Fasten the return spring)

4-2

Printed in Japan
A0A5055-JC03

Chapter 4 Reassembling and Servicing of Drive Unit
1. Swivel/Steering Bracket
_____SM/D27A & D36A

f. Install the assembly to the half tilt arm (A).
Install the half tilt spring (and the stopper) to the hook. (Option)

g. Install the tilt stop rod to the tilt stop lever.
Install the shock absorber to the swivel bracket. Install the spring and the tilt stop rod to the absorber lever.

h. Install the steering brake cover, brake spring and collar to the swivel bracket in that order, and temporarily tighten them with brake bolts. (The steering load must be adjusted after installing.)

(Shock absorber)

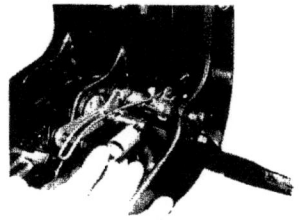

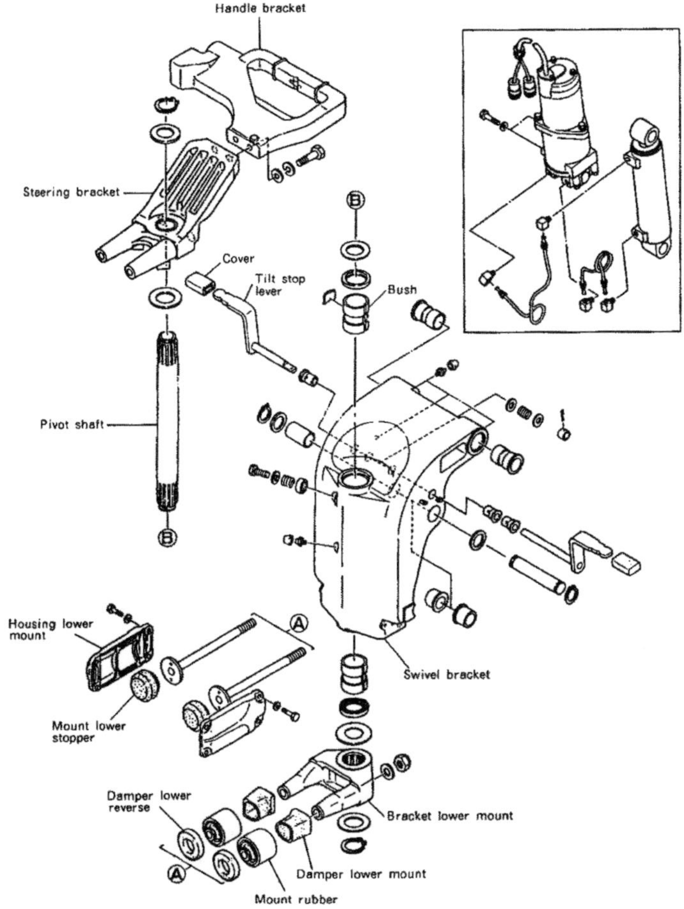

Handle bracket

Steering bracket

Cover

Tilt stop lever

Bush

Pivot shaft

Housing lower mount

Mount lower stopper

Swivel bracket

Damper lower reverse

Bracket lower mount

Damper lower mount

Mount rubber

Printed in Japan
A0A5055-JC03

2. Clamp Bracket

The left and right clamp brackets, which are made of aluminum, make a pair. They are bolted to the transom.

1. Cautions when reassembling and servicing

    (1) Clamp bracket

    a. Install the clamp bracket assembly to the swivel bracket, and set the left and right assemblies with the tilt tube and support bolt. Install the assembly either to the shock absorber or to the support bolt of the hydraulic cylinder.

(Clamp bracket)

Tilt tube nut tightening torque	2.0kgf-m

b. Install the thrust rod.

c. Check the tilt-up load (tilting start position at molding), and the tilt-up angle (angle to the transom plate). Also check the half-tilt function.

(Tilt tube hole)

	Standard
Tilt-up load	<25kg
Tilt-up angle	76°

NOTE: Apply grease to the bearing parts of the tilt tube and the shock absorber.

    Recommended grease:
        COSMO GREASE DYNAMAX EP No.2
        or equivalent

(Install to the swivel bracket)

(Set left and right clamp bracket with tilt tube)

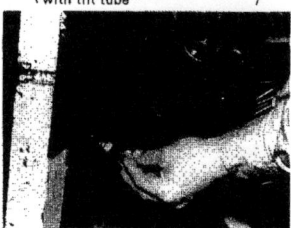
(Support bolt bush)

3. Upper Case

The upper case, which is made of aluminum die casting, consists of the upper and the lower part. The upper case includes cooling water passage in a caste holes, exhaust tube mounting part (in a recessed part) and the drive shaft.

1. Cautions when reassembling and servicing

    (1) Install the screw plug, nozzle (cooling water) and the seal rubber plug (M8 X 8) to the upper case.
    (2) Install the mount rubber assembly to the upper case with a bracket.

Bolt(M8×60) tightening torque	Width(12) 1.9~2.1kgf-m

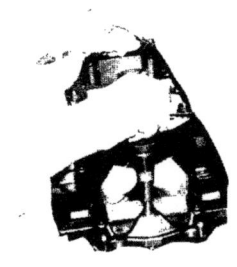
(Engine mount)

    (3) Install the upper case made in (1) above and the mount rubber assembly to the steering bracket. Do not forget to fit a bend washer.

U-nut (M10) tightening torque	Width(14) 3.7~3.9kgf-m

    (4) Install the exhaust pipe to the upper case.

Bolt (M6×20) tightening torque	Width (10) 0.7~0.9kgf-m

(Install the exhaust pipe)

    (5) Install the LO tube.
    (6) Install the oil dipstick and the level tube.
    (7) Insert the water seal rubber into the seal rubber case, and install the seal rubber case and anti-corrosive zinc.
    (8) Check the vibration-proof mount rubber
        If the vibration-proof mount rubber is hardened or cracked, replace it.
    (9) Check the rubber boot
        If there are any cracks on the rubber boot, replace it.

(Install the vibration-proof mount rubber)

Chapter 4 Reassembling and Servicing of Drive Unit
4. Bottom Cowling and Fitting Parts   SM/D27A & D36A

4. Bottom Cowling and Fitting Parts

The fuel pipe, battery cable, steering cable outlet, key-switch and stop lever are installed with seal rubbers to the front of the floating connection of the upper case.

1. Cautions when reassembling and servicing

   (1) Fuel pipe and battery cable
       Install fuel pipes and battery cables as specified, seal them with a waterproof grommet, and secure them with clamps.

   (2) Stop lever load
       Check the stop lever load after connecting the cable.

Stop lever load (standard)	$5 \sim 7$ kgf-m

   (3) Apply grease to the stop lever bearing parts, spring and the cable connection.

Recommended grease	COSMO GREASE DYNAMAX EP No.2 or the equivalent

   (4) Connecting the bottom cowling and the upper case
       Install the bottom cowling to the upper case shift bracket.

Bolt (M6×40) tightening torque	Width ⑩ $0.7 \sim 0.9$ kgf-m

   (5) Install the shift bracket to the upper case.

Tightening torque M6×25	Width ⑩ $0.7 \sim 0.9$ kgf-m

   (6) Check the seal rubber.
       Air-tightness will be lost if there are any cracks or inelasticity with the rubber. In such cases, replace the seal rubber.

(Connect the bottom cowling)

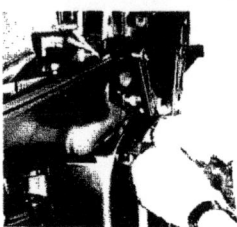
(Install the shift handle)

(Install the harness holder)

(Fuel connecting part)

Chapter 4 Reassembling and Servicing of Drive Unit
4. Bottom Cowling and Fitting Parts

SM/D27A & D36A

(7) Check the cable.
Replace the cable if the connector is worn or damaged, the insulation is damaged or the function is faulty due to rusting.

(Harness)

(Stop cable and regulator rod)

(8) Shift device
The shift lever shaft, the reverse limit shaft and the safety switch are installed on the bracket (shift). The input power is transmitted through the shift rod connection to the drive shaft.

1) Function

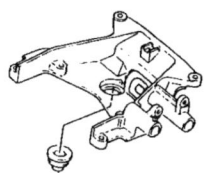
(Shift bracket for D36A)

Forward	When the shift handle is shifted to forward, the shift rod and the shift cam rod are moved up and down through the detent shift, and the shift cam pushes the dog clutch forward. The input power is thus transmitted to the propeller shaft via the pinion.
Reverse	When the shift handle is shifted to reverse, the dog clutch engages with the reverse gear to transmit reverse rotation to the propeller shaft.
Neutral	In neutral, both the reverse and the forward gears turn idly, and the propeller shaft does not turn.

2) Cautions when reassembling and servicing

a. Operation force of shift handle
(The following should be done after installing the lower case assembly.)
After installing the shift device, check the operation force of the shift handle.

	Standard
Shift handle operation force	ℓ =55mm position 2~7kgf-m

b. Apply grease to the bearing parts of the shift lever shaft and the bracket (stopper).

Recommended grease	COSMO GREASE DYNAMAX EP No.2 or the equivalent

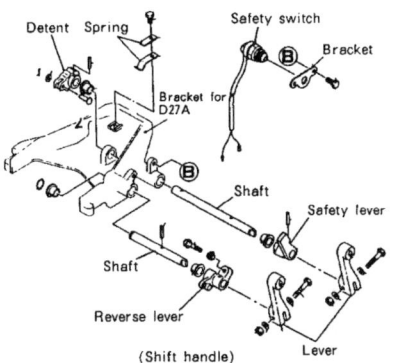
(Shift handle)

Chapter 4 Reassembling and Servicing of Drive Unit
4. Bottom Cowling and Fitting Parts   *SM/D27A & D36A*

c. Apply grease to the bearing parts of the reverse limit shaft and the bracket (shift).

d. Shift cam rod
- Install the guide, O-ring (1AP21), washer (6.5), O-ring (6) and washer (6) to the shift cam rod, and fix the shift cam with a pin.
- Install the shift cam rod assembly to the lower case, and tighten the shift rod guide to the lower case.

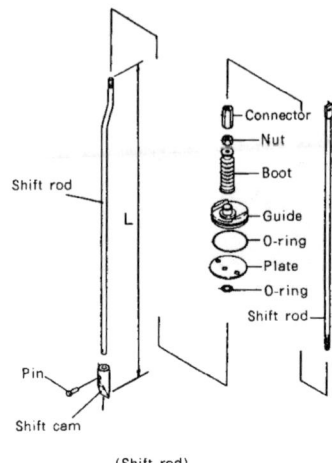

Bolt (M6 × 20) tightening torque	Width ⑩ 0.7~0.9kgf-m

e. Adjusting shift rod
Push down the shift cam rod to the lowermost position, and connect the shift rod while shifting the detent of the shift rod end to the reverse position.

f. Adjusting shift rod boot
Check the length of the shift rod boot when it is shifted to the reverse position.

	Standard
Shift rod boot length	39.4~43.5mm

NOTE: 1. Use new O-ring (6) (1AP21) and boot.
2. Apply THREE BOND #1215 to bolts and nuts.

g. Safety switch
Install the safety switch to the shift bracket.

Bolt (M6 × 16) tightening torque	Width ⑩ 0.7~0.9kgf-m

Chapter 4 Reassembling and Servicing of Drive Unit
5. Lower Gear Case

5. Lower Gear Case

- The lower gear case is an integrated lube-oil-sealed-type gear case. A self-adjusting type anti-corrosive zinc is on the trim tab.
- A resin strainer is attached to the cooling water inlet on the bottom of the cavitation plate.
- The shift rod is sealed with a boot and an O-ring. The oil guide is provided on the lower periphery of the drive shaft.

(Upper part of lower gear case)

1. Reassembling and servicing

   (1) Forward gear

   a. Install the bearing outer race and the shim to the lower gear case.

   b. Install the forward gear and the bearing (30207).

	Standard
Clearance between gear outside dia. and bearing inside dia. (tightening margin)	0.002~0.030mm

   c. Install the forward gear and bearing assembly to the lower gear case.

(Lower part of lower gear case)

	Standard
Clearance between lower gear case hole and bearing outside dia.	-0.021~0.022mm

   (2) Drive shaft and pinion

   a. Install the needle (BH-1616) to the lower gear case.

	Standard
Clearance between needle inside dia. and drive shaft dia.	0.001~0.064mm

   (Press in the punched side of the bearing.)

   b. Install the thrust bearing (AZ254211) to the drive shaft.

(Reassembling and servicing)

	Standard
Clearance between shaft outside dia. and bearing inside dia. (tightening margin)	0.002~0.033mm

   (Fix only one side of the race plate.)

   c. Insert the oil guide through the upper part of the lower gear case. (For insertion, align the top end notch of the oil guide with the hole groove of the lower gear case.)

(Lower gear case assembly)

Chapter 4 Reassembling and Servicing of Drive Unit
5. Lower Gear Case   SM/D27A & D36A

d. Insert the drive shaft through the upper part of the lower gear case.

e. Install the pinion to the spline which is at the lower end of the drive shaft.

Stop nut (M12 thin) tightening torque	Width (19) $9.5^{\pm 0.5}$ kgf-m

f. Install the shift cam rod. Refer to P. 4-8.

(3) Oil seal case

a. Install the needle (HK2520) to the lower part of the oil seal case.

	Standard
Clearance between needle inside dia. and drive shaft dia.	0.003~0.065mm

b. Install the oil seal (SC25378), spacer and oil seal (SC25378) to the upper part of the oil seal case in that order.

NOTE: 1. Fill grease between the oil seals.

Recommended grease : OIL CENTER RESEARCH LOR#101
Filling quantity : 20 to 30% of the space volume

2. Be careful not to install the oil seal in the wrong position.

c. Install the shim set and the thrust bearing (AZ254211) to the lower part of the oil seal case.

(For adjusting, refer to p. 9-1.)

	Standard
Clearance between bearing outside dia. and oil seal case inside dia.	0~0.041mm

(Fix only one side of the race plate.)

d. Install the oil seal case lower assembly to the lower gear case via the upper end of the drive shaft.

NOTE: 1. Use new O-ring (1AG45).
2. Apply THREE BOND #1215 to the joining surfaces of the oil case and the lower gear case.

e. Check the clearance of the drive shaft direction. Measure the clearance with the special jig, regarding the lower surface of the pinion gear as zero level. Adjust the clearance with the shim set.

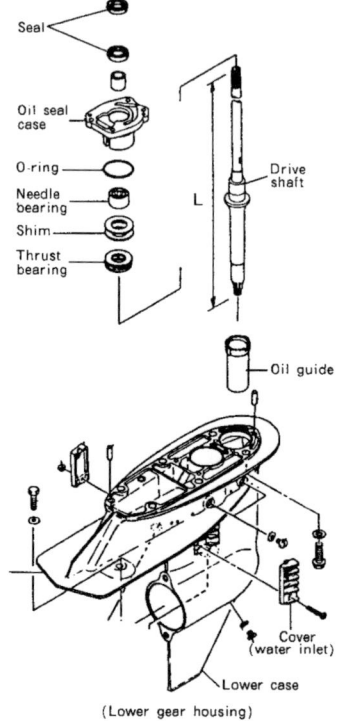

(Lower gear housing)

Chapter 4 Reassembling and Servicing of Drive Unit
5. Lower Gear Case

_____SM/D27A & D36A

(4) Bearing housing

a. Install the oil seal (SC20307), spacer, and oil seal (SC20307) in that order to the rear part of the bearing housing.

NOTE: 1. Fill grease between the oil seals.
  Recommended grease : OIL CENTER RESEARCH LOR#101
  Filling quantity : 20 to 30% of the space volume
2. Be careful not to install the oil seal in the wrong position.

(Bearing housing and oil seal case)

b. Push the needle (20NQ3315D) into the front part of the bearing housing, and install a stop ring.

	Standard
Clearance between needle outside dia. and housing inside dia. (tightening margin)	0.011~0.047mm

NOTE: The shaft center inclination with the needle installed must be below $50\mu/100mm$.

(5) Reverse gear and bearing

a. Install the bearing (6008) to the reverse gear.

(Bearing housing)

	Standard
Clearance between gear outside dia. and bearing inside dia. (tightening margin)	0.002~0.030mm

(6) Propeller shaft and clutch

a. Insert the shaft spring into the front end hole of the propeller shaft, and fit the dog clutch into the spline.
b. Align the dog clutch cross pin hole with the propeller shaft groove hole, and insert a cross pin.
c. Fit a cross pin ring to the periphery of the dog clutch cross pin hole.
d. Install the shift plunger to the front end hole in the propeller shaft.

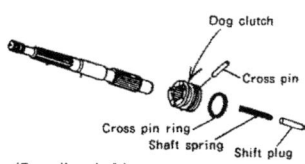

(Propeller shaft)

(7) Propeller shaft assembly and bearing housing assembly

a. Install the propeller shaft assembly to the bearing housing assembly.
b. Install the propeller shaft and the bearing housing assembly to the lower gear case.

Bolt (M10 × 35) tightening torque	Width ⑭ $3.8^{\pm 0.1}$kgf-m

NOTE: 1. Apply THREE BOND #1215 to the threads of the bolt (M10 X 35).
2. Use new O-ring (1AG75).

(Install the propeller shaft to the bearing housing)

Chapter 4 Reassembling and Servicing of Drive Unit
5. Lower Gear Case

SM/D27A & D36A

c. Check the backlash between the forward gear and the pinion.
(Measure the backlash while pushing the drive shaft pinion upward, and adjust the backlash using the shim on the forward gear side.)
Push the propeller shaft in the direction of the forward thrust using a jig, and measure the backlash. Do the same procedures for the reverse gear.

	Standard
Backlash between forward gear and pinion	0.1~0.25mm
Backlash between reverse gear and pinion	0.1~0.4mm

(Measuring jig for backlash between forward gear and pinion)

Refer to p. 9-1 (forward gear) and p. 9-2 (reverse gear).

NOTE: Adjust the backlash keeping the adjusting shim away from oil and other contamination.

Spline sleeve A (196640-92950)

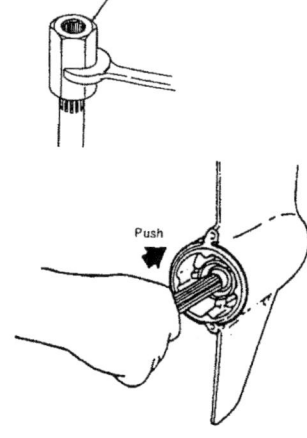

d. Check the gear contact pattern for pinion and forward gear.
Apply red lead to the contact surface of the forward gear, and install the propeller shaft and other related parts to the gear case.
When installing the propeller shaft, fix it manually so that it does not turn. Turn the drive shaft slowly about 5 times with a special tool A, remove the forward gear from the propeller shaft, and check that the gear contact is proper.

Gear contact pattern

The forward gear contacts partially during rotation as shown in the illustration. From the contact pattern, you can judge whether or not the gear contact positions are proper.

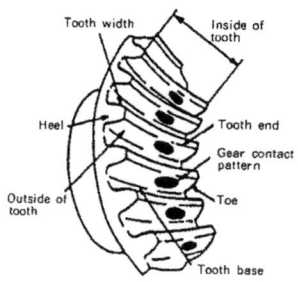

Chapter 4 Reassembling and Servicing of Drive Unit
5. Lower Gear Case

The ideal gear contact pattern is shown below. This pattern is obtained by adjusting shim.

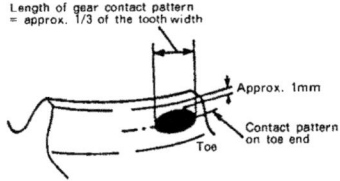

The illustration on the right shows the contact pattern on the toe end. In this case, reduce the shim thickness at the forward gear, and increase the shim thickness at the pinion gear.

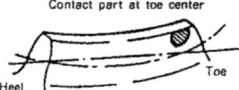

NOTE: Gear contact at the toe end causes damage to the forward gear and the tooth base of the pinion gear. The gear contact pattern must be avoided.

If the gear contact pattern is at the tooth base as shown in the illustration on the right, increase the shim thickness at the forward gear and reduce the shim thickness at the pinion gear slightly to obtain the ideal gear contact pattern.

(Gear contact at tooth base)

NOTE: Improper gear contact position causes damage to pinion gear tooth. Be sure to adjust the gear contact in such cases.

e. Check the reverse gear contact pattern.
Do the same procedures as for checking forward gear contact pattern, except that you must pull the propeller shaft as shown on the right diagram.

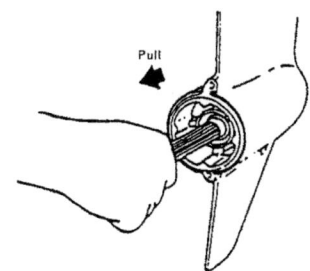

Chapter 4 Reassembling and Servicing of Drive Unit
5. Lower Gear Case

SM/D27A & D36A

f. Check the clearance of the propeller shaft.
(Refer to P. 9-2 for adjusting procedure.)

	Standard
Propeller shaft direction clearance	0.3~0.5mm

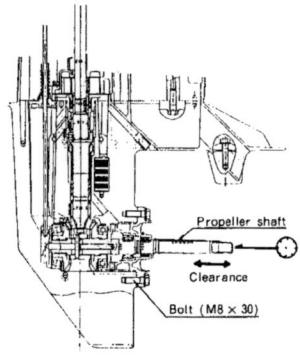

(Measuring propeller shaft clearance)

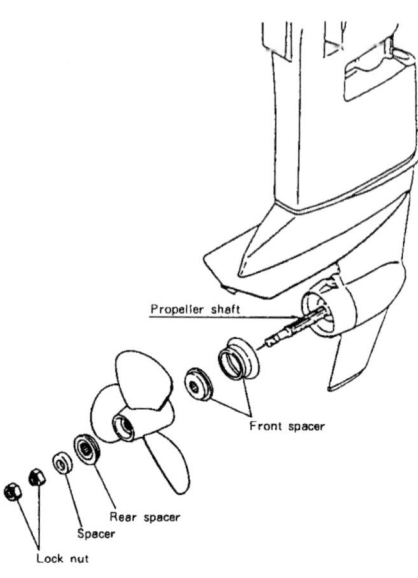

(8) Propeller
   a. Install the front spacer, propeller and rear spacer in that order.
   b. Tighten the propeller nuts.

Propeller nut M16 tightening torque	Nut A	$3.5^{\pm 0.5}$ kgf-m
	Nut B	$4.0^{\pm 0.5}$ kgf-m

NOTE: Apply grease to the outside circumference of the propeller shaft, the inside circumference of the propeller and the threads of the propeller nut.

Recommended grease :
    COSMO GREASE DYNAMAX EP No.2

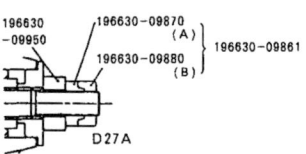

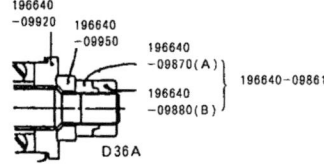

Chapter 4 Reassembling and Servicing of Drive Unit
6. Cooling Water Pump and Cooling Water Piping

6. Cooling Water Pump and Cooling Water Piping

1. Cooling water pump
   a. Install the gasket and the outer plate in alignment with the positioning parallel pin (6 X 11) on the oil seal case.
   b. Install the semi-circular key and the impeller. (Be careful of the orientation of the impeller blades when installing the impeller.)
   c. Install the insert.
   d. Align the housing with the positioning parallel pin (6 X 11), and install it on the oil seal case.

Bolt (M6 × 40) tightening torque	Width (⑪) 0.7~0.9kgf-m

   e. Attach the anti-corrosive zinc and the installation plate, and tighten the bolts.

2. Cooling water piping
   a. Install the rubber and the tube to the cooling water pump housing, and fasten the guide (B).

Tapping screw (M5 × 12) tightening torque	⊕torque screwdriver

   b. Insert the upper end of the cooling water tube into the upper hole of the upper case.

3. Cautions when reassembling and servicing
   a. Check the clearance in the impeller shaft direction.

	Standard
Clearance in impeller shaft direction	0~0.5mm

   b. Be careful of the position of the impeller blades when installing.
   c. Apply grease to the impeller.

Recommended grease	COSMO GREASE DYNAMAX EP №2 or the equivalent

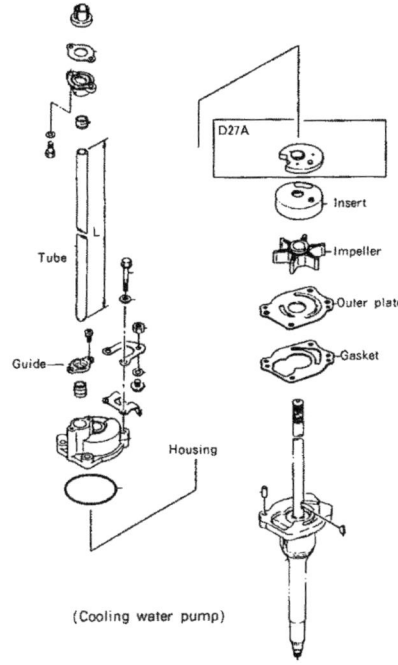

(Cooling water pump)

7. Steering Handle

The steering handle is made of aluminum. The engine speed can be controlled by turning the grip. The handle is foldable and is connected to the regulator handle on the engine via the regulator cable with a brake.

1. Cautions when reassembling and servicing

   (1) Grip load
   Apply grease to the inner bearing part of the grip.
   Adjust the load with the brake bolt (M6 X 20).

   (2) Steering turning angle
   Check the steering turning angle.

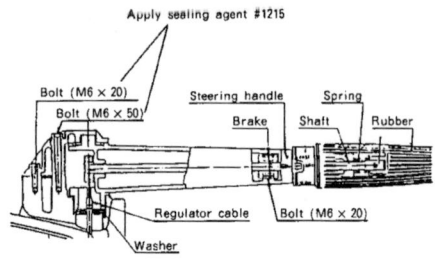

Steering turning angle (identical for left and right; standard)	38° ~ 42°

   (3) Steering handle lifting load
   Check the steering handle lifting load.

Handle lifting load (standard)	0.25~0.45kgf

   (4) Apply grease to the inner bearing parts of the grip and the steering.

Recommended grease	COSMO GREASE DYNAMAX EP No.2 or the equivalent

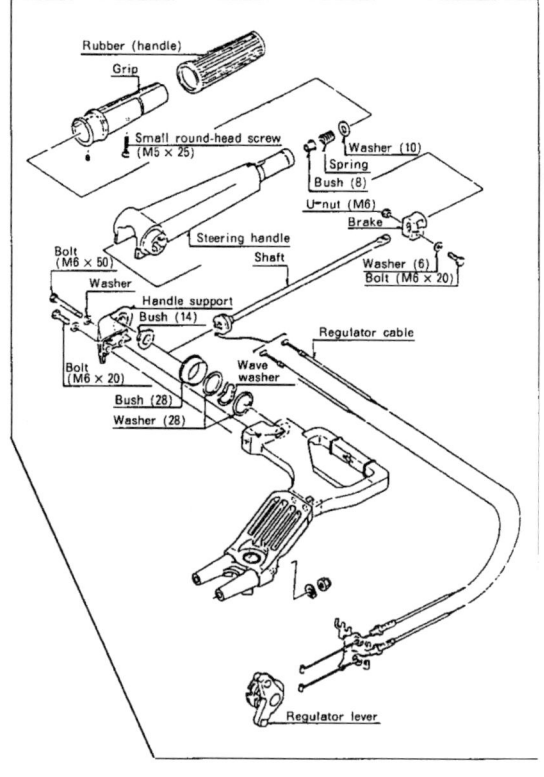

8. Hydraulic Cylinder

1. Insert 2 bushes (18/24 X 20) into the swivel bracket.
2. Insert 1 bush (18/24 X 40) into the hydraulic cylinder.
3. Install and secure the hydraulic cylinder to the swivel bracket with the pin.
4. Install the washer and stop ring C.
5. Apply sealing agent to the taper screw plug and install it.

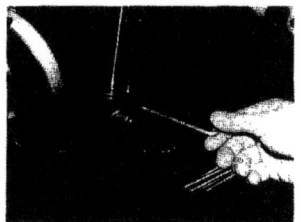
(Install the taper screw plug)

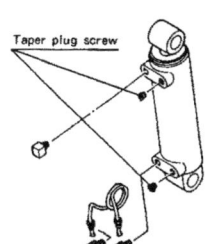

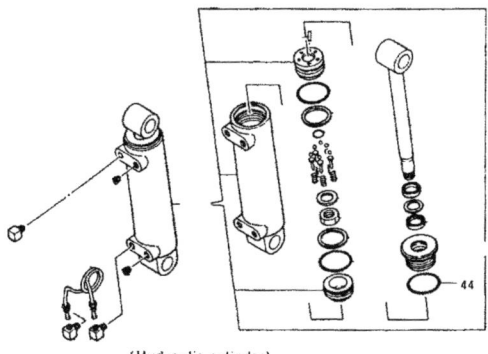
(Hydraulic cylinder)

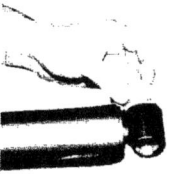
(Insert 2 bushes)

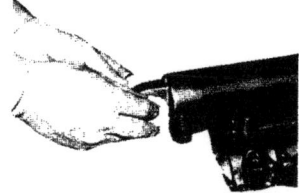
(Insert 1 bush)

(Install the washer)

(Install the stop ring C)

9. Electric-hydraulic Tilting

(1) Electric-hydraulic power unit

Specifications	
Power unit type	PU-3
Motor	12V 400W (nominal output)
Hydraulic pump (gear type)	0.35cc/rev (theoretical delivery volume)
Power tilt oil	ATF-A (COSMO)
Oil capacity	Approximately 0.24 ℓ
Tilt-up time	7 sec. (temp. 20°C)

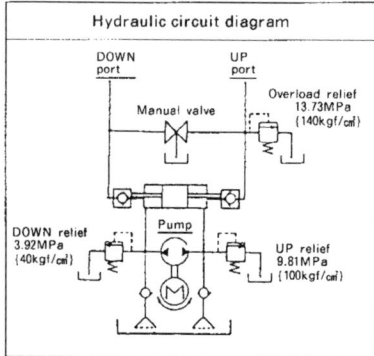

Hydraulic circuit diagram

NOTE: Fill hydraulic oil up to the filling port with the unit tilted up to the maximum.

(Piping)

(Install the power unit)

(Pass coupler through grommet hole)

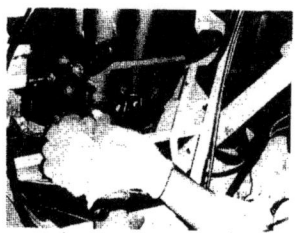

(Install the seal tape and the flare adaptor)

(Install the flare tube)

Chapter 4 Reassembling snd Servicing of Drive Unit
9. Electric-hydraulic Tilting
_SM/D27A & D36A_

(2) Procedures for supplying power unit oil

1) Remove the plug from the (A) part.

2) Tilt up and down 4 to 5 times while supplying oil through the plug hole using an oil filler.

3) When the oil stops entering, fill oil up to the plug hole at the tilt-up position, and tighten the plug. When changing oil, remove the power unit, and pour out the oil from the (A) part. However, changing oil is almost unnecessary, because the oil hardly deteriorates.

(3) Procedures for power tilt manual operation

If the engine cannot be tilted up or down due to a trouble, turn counter clockwise (loosen) the manual valve on the (B) part with a ⊖ screwdriver to open both the down side and the lap side of the hydraulic circuit. Then the engine can be tilted up or down manually. In this case, lock the engine in the tilted position with the manual tilt lock lever. (The manual tilt lock lever is used only in case of emergency.)

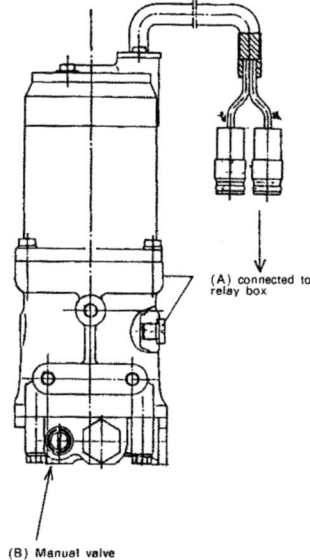

(A) connected to relay box

(B) Manual valve

Chapter 4 Reassembling and Servicing of Drive Unit
10. Connecting the Upper Case with Steering Bracket

10. Connecting the Upper Case with Steering Bracket

The upper case and the steering bracket are bolted together through the mount rubber. They are bolted at two points: upper and lower. The upper point is the steering bracket with stopper brackets (left and right brackets differ in shape), and the lower point is the lower mount bracket with the damper.

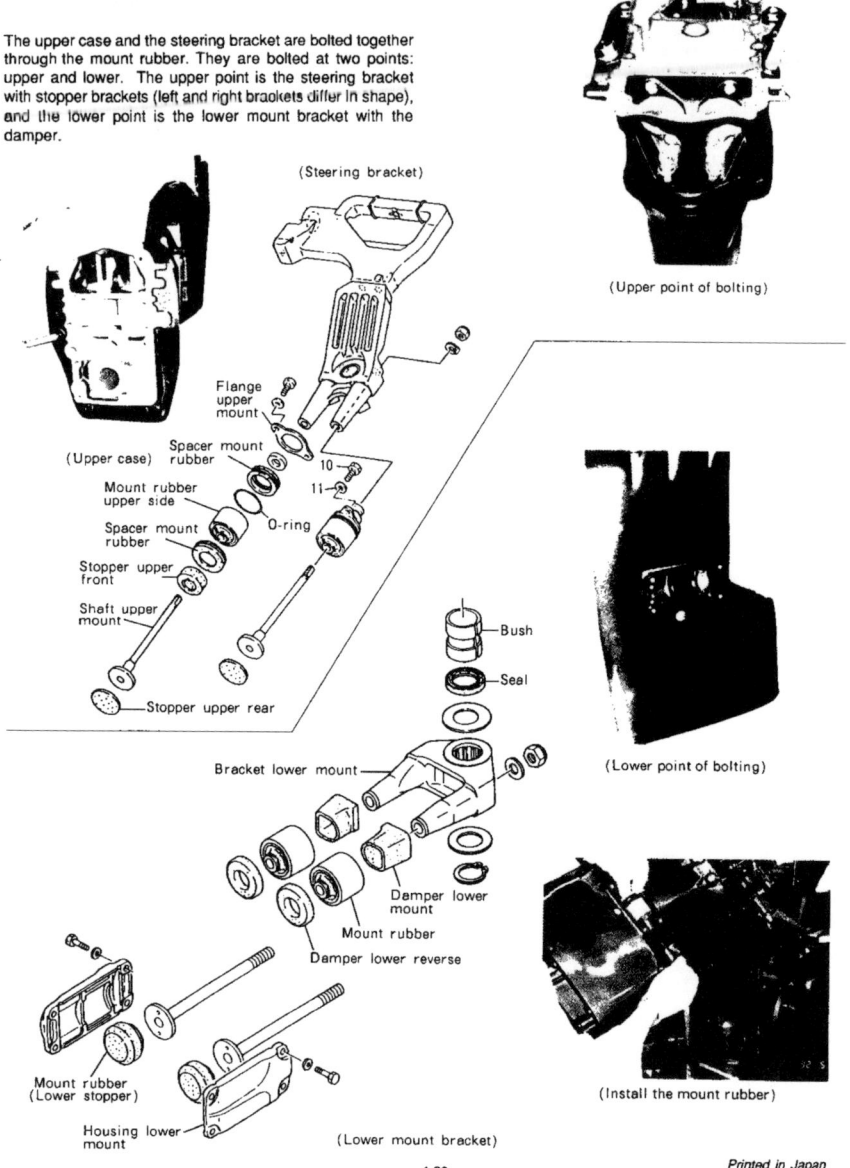

CHAPTER 5
PIPING DIAGRAM

1. Piping Diagram 5-1

Chapter 5 Piping Diagram
1. Piping Diagram   SM/D27A & D36A

1. Piping Diagram

(1) D27A

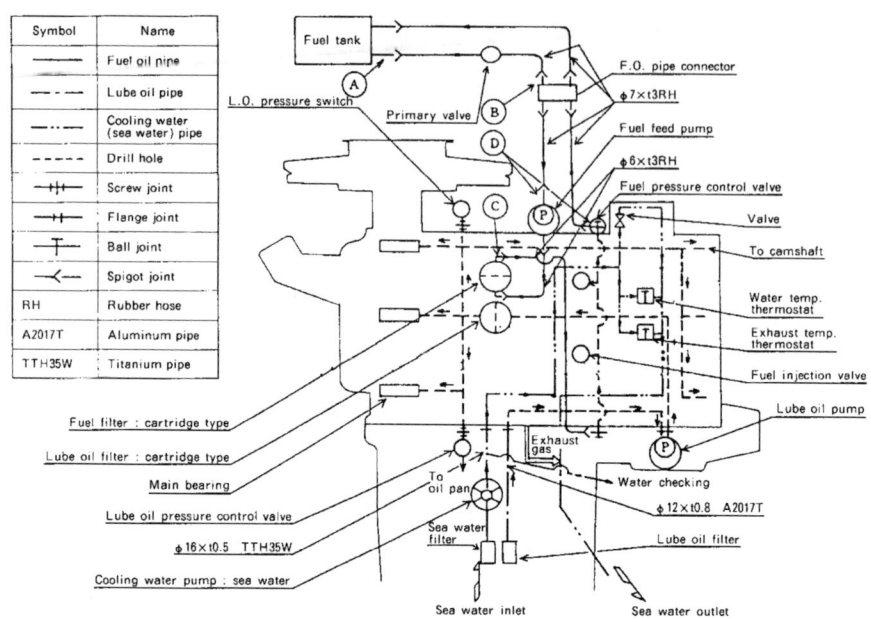

Symbol	Name
——	Fuel oil pipe
— - - —	Lube oil pipe
— ·· —	Cooling water (sea water) pipe
- - - -	Drill hole
—+++—	Screw joint
—++—	Flange joint
—T—	Ball joint
—<—	Spigot joint
RH	Rubber hose
A2017T	Aluminum pipe
TTH35W	Titanium pipe

Thermostat valve opening temp.

Water temp. thermostat	72°C	82°C
Exhaust temp. thermostat	65°C	75°C

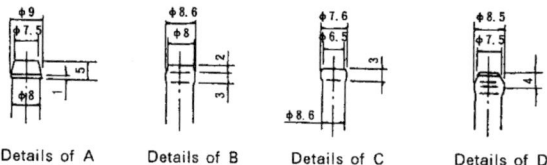

Details of A   Details of B   Details of C   Details of D

NOTE: The pipe dimensions in the diagram above show inner diameter X thickness for rubber pipes and
outer diameter X thickness for other pipes.

Chapter 5 Piping Diagram
1. Piping Diagram

(2) D36A

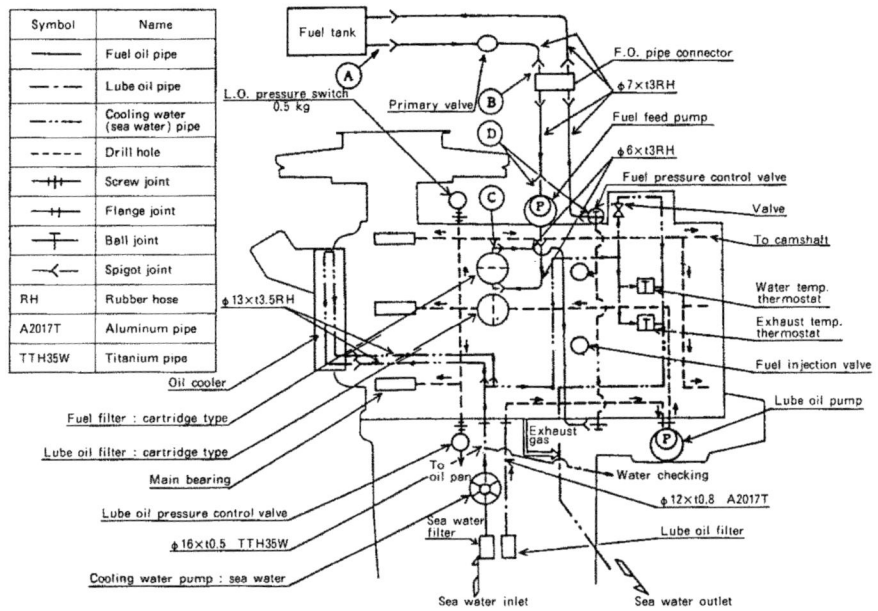

Thermostat valve opening temp.

Water temp. thermostat	72°C	82°C
Exhaust temp. thermostat	65°C	75°C

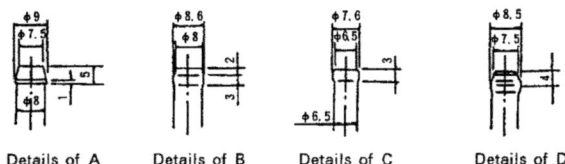

| Details of A | Details of B | Details of C | Details of D |

NOTE: The pipe dimensions in the diagram above show inner diameter X thickness for rubber pipes and outer diameter X thickness for other pipes.

CHAPTER 6
ELECTRIC EQUIPMENT

1. Generator 6-1
2. Starting Motor (Reduction Gear) 6-2
3. Warning Device 6-4
4. Wiring Diagram 6-6

Chapter 6 Electric Equipment
1. Generator   SM/D27A & D36A

1. Generator

1. Specifications

Type	K6055 made by KOKUSAN DENKI
YANMAR code No.	120380-77221
Charging specification	Full wave rectification, battery load
Charging current	10 ± 0.5A at 14V, N=3600 r.p.m. (at normal temperature)
Charging start speed	Less than 1000 r.p.m. at battery voltage 13V
Ambient temperature	-20°C ~ +65°C
Direction of rotation	Clockwise (viewed from flywheel side)
Weight	Approximately 1.1kg

NOTE: Apply screw lock to the rotor mounting bolt (M6 X 22) before installing.

2. Regulator

Type	SU243Y made by KOKUSAN DENKI
Control system	AC half-wave short-circuit control
YANMAR code No.	120380-77720-1
Combination load	Lamp load : 13.0V 40W
Combination load	Battery : 12.0V 70AH (full charge)
Weight	150g

(Install the regulator)

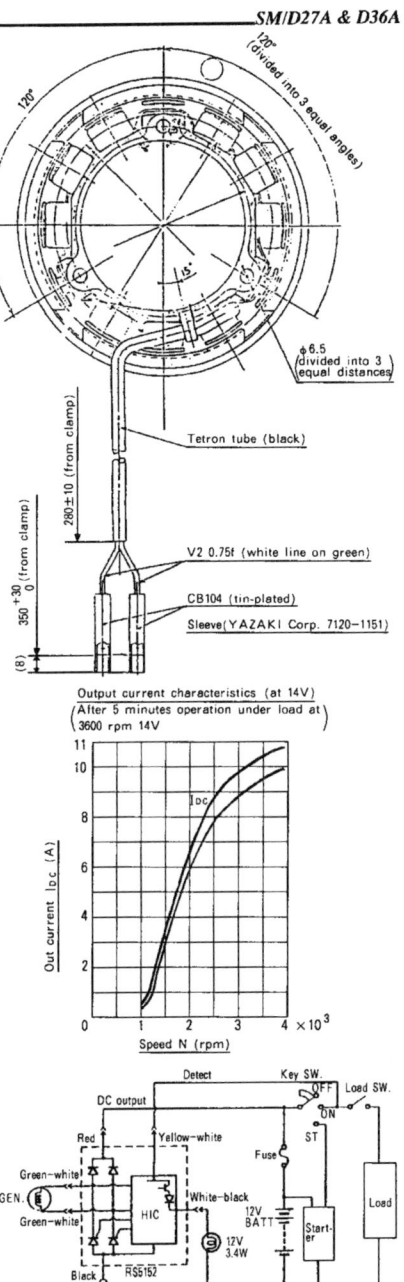

Printed in Japan
A0A5055-JC03

6-1

Chapter 6 Electric Equipment
2. Starting Motor (Reduction Gear)

SM/D27A & D36A

2. Starting Motor (Reduction Gear)

1. Specifications

1) D27A

Type		S114-451A made by HITACHI	
YANMAR code No.		120370-77011	
Nominal output		1.2kW	
Circuit voltage		12V	
Rating		30sec	
Direction of rotation		Counterclockwise (viewed from pinion side)	
Circuit system		Body grounding	
Clutch system		Roller clutch	
Pinion	Number of teeth	9	Tooth end diameter ϕ29.6
	Pressure angle	20°	Pitch circle diameter ϕ22.86
	Shift quantity	1.27	Tooth bottom diameter ϕ20.7
	Hardness	HRC58~63	Double-sheathed tooth thickness 12.49⁻⁰·¹²
Pinion shift system		Torsion spring system	
Weight		4.3	

2) D36A

Type		S114-477 made by HITACHI	
YANMAR code No.		120380-77010	
Nominal output		1.4kW	
Circuit voltage		12V	
Rating		30sec	
Direction of rotation		Counterclockwise (viewed from pinion side)	
Circuit system		Body grounding	
Clutch system		Roller clutch	
Pinion	Number of teeth	9	Tooth end diameter ϕ29.6
	Pressure angle	20°	Pitch circle diameter ϕ22.86
	Shift quantity	1.27	Tooth bottom diameter ϕ20.7
	Hardness	HRC58~63	Double-sheathed tooth thickness 12.4⁻⁰·¹²
Pinion shift system		Torsion spring system	
Weight		4.6	

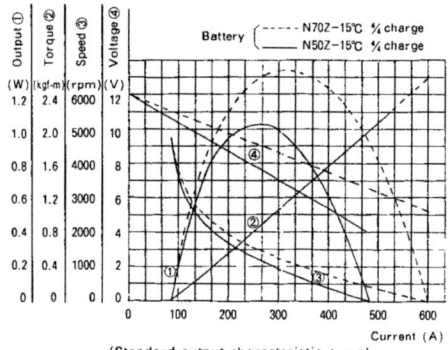

(Standard output characteristic curve)

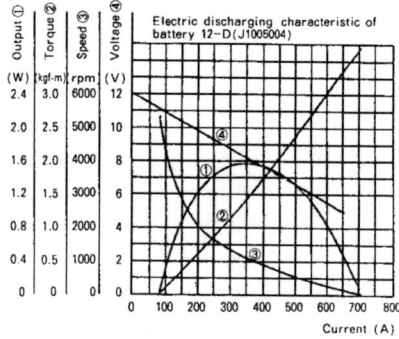

(Standard output characteristic curve)

Chapter 6 Electric Equipment
2. Starting Motor (Reduction Gear)

2. Structure and functions

(1) Starter
The reduction gear is placed between the armature and the pinion, and the motor torque is increased and transmitted to the pinion.

(2) Reduction gear
The small gear installed on the armature shaft tip always engages with the large gear on the clutch circumference, and the rotation of the armature is transmitted through the reduction gear and the clutch to the pinion.

(3) Pinion shift system
The pinion shift system is a torsion spring system. The system consists of an outer clutch, a roller and an inner clutch. The clutch is fixed with a ball bearing, and the pinion shaft is pushed into the inside of the inner clutch through the helical spline, causing the pinion to engage with the ring gear.

(4) Roller clutch
The roller clutch consists of a roller, an inner clutch and an outer clutch. The roller is always pushed by the spring, and retained in the direction of the shorter dimension of the outer clutch. When the roller turns in the direction of the longer dimension of the outer clutch, the outer clutch rotates idly. When the roller turns in the narrow direction of the taper, the clutch inner and outer combine and transmit the rotation.

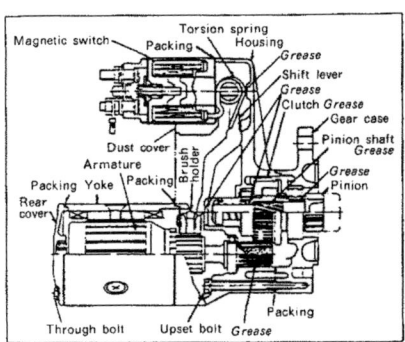

(Structural diagram)

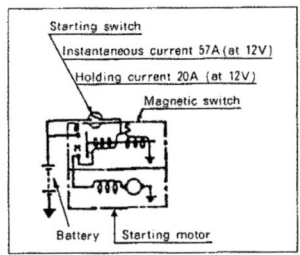

(Starting motor wiring diagram)

3. Warning Device

1. Details of warning device

    (1) The alarm buzzer turns ON from abnormality such as insufficient hydraulic pressure, overheat or poor battery charge.
    (2) The alarm lamp turns on from insufficient hydraulic pressure only. If the alarm lamp is OFF and the alarm buzzer is ON, the cause is overheat or poor battery charge.

(Standard specifications)

	Alarm buzzer	Alarm lamp
Insufficient hydraulic pressure	○	○
Overheat	○	—
Battery charge	○	—
Installing place	Arbitrary $\ell = 3$ m from bottom cowling	Standard position on bottom cowling

(Option)
For Type B (p. 6-8) and Type C (p. 6-9)

	Alarm buzzer	Alarm lamp
Insufficient hydraulic pressure	○	○
Overheat	○	○
Battery charge	○	○
Installing place	Indicator panel	

Chapter 6 Electric Equipment
3. Warning Device

2. Functioning of warning device

    (1) Turning key switch ON causes the alarm buzzer and the alarm lamp to turn ON for approximately 2 sec.

    (2) If you leave the key switch without starting the engine for approximately 180 sec., the buzzer and the lamp turn ON again. When you start the engine after that, the buzzer and the lamp turn OFF.

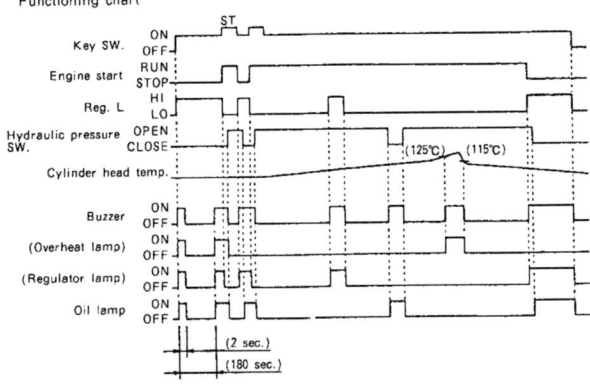

Functioning chart

Chapter 6 Electric Equipment
4. Wiring Diagram

4. Wiring Diagram

(1) Wiring diagram of standard type with warning device

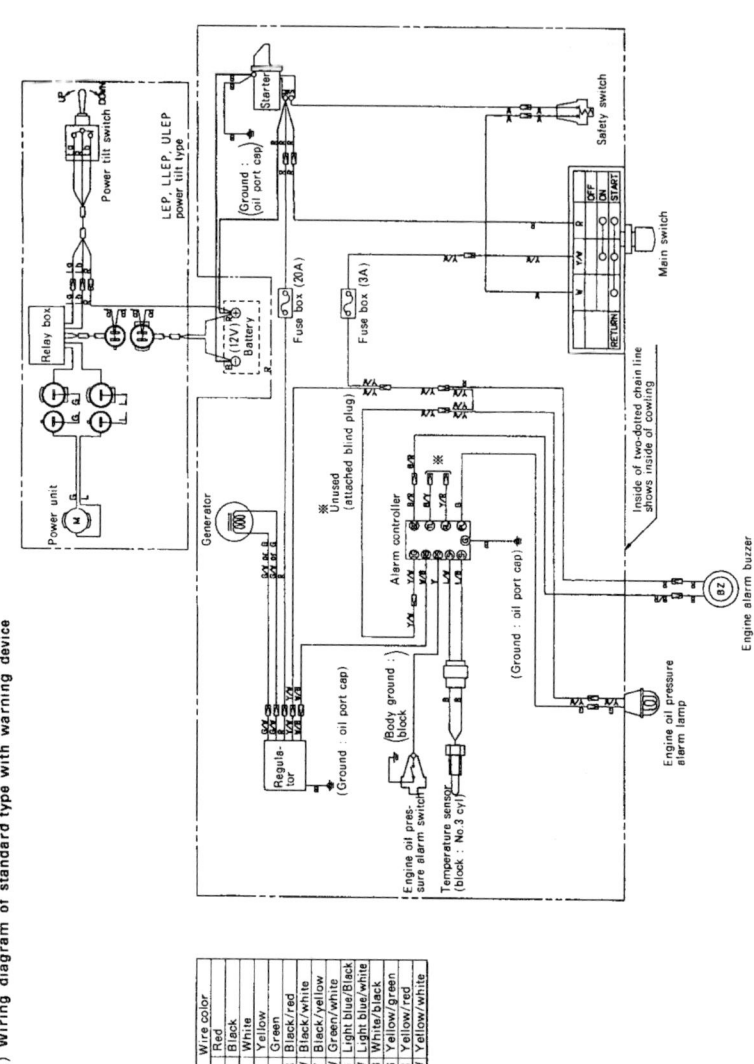

	Wire color
R	Red
B	Black
W	White
Y	Yellow
G	Green
B/R	Black/red
B/W	Black/white
B/Y	Black/yellow
G/W	Green/white
L/B	Light blue/black
L/W	Light blue/white
W/B	White/black
Y/G	Yellow/green
Y/R	Yellow/red
Y/W	Yellow/white

Chapter 6 Electric Equipment
4. Wiring Diagram _____ *SM/D27A & D36A*

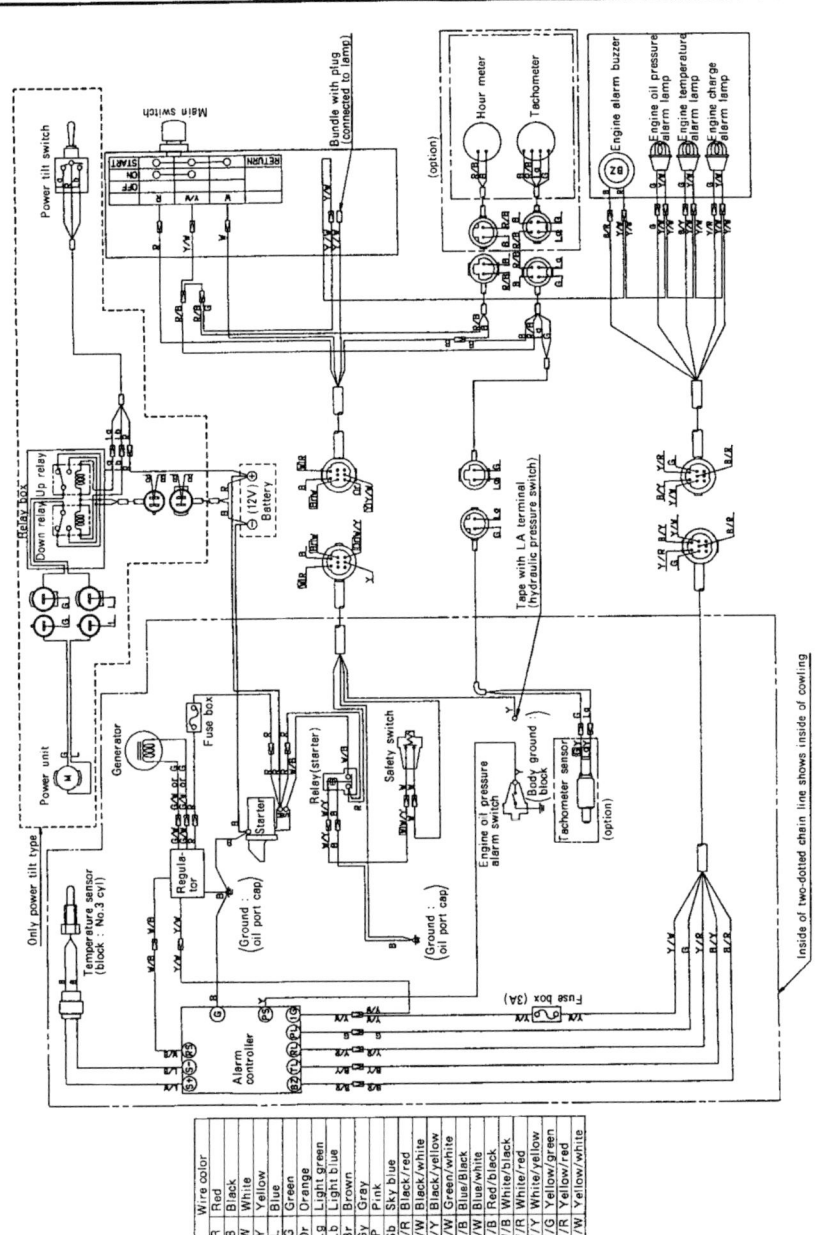

(2) Wiring diagram of type A with warning device

6-7

Printed in Japan
A0A5055-JC03

Chapter 6 Electric Equipment
4. Wiring Diagram

SM/D27A & D36

(3) Wiring diagram of type B with warning device

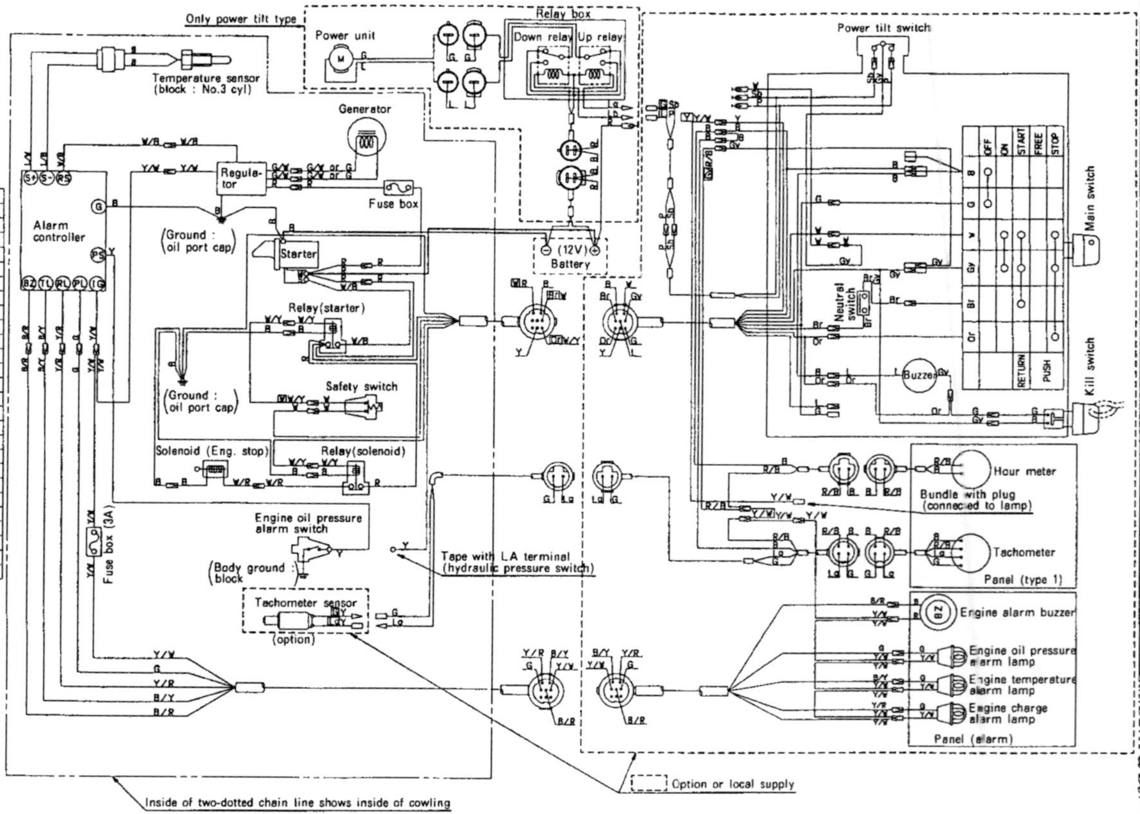

Chapter 6 Electric Equipment
4. Wiring Diagram

SM/D27A & D36A

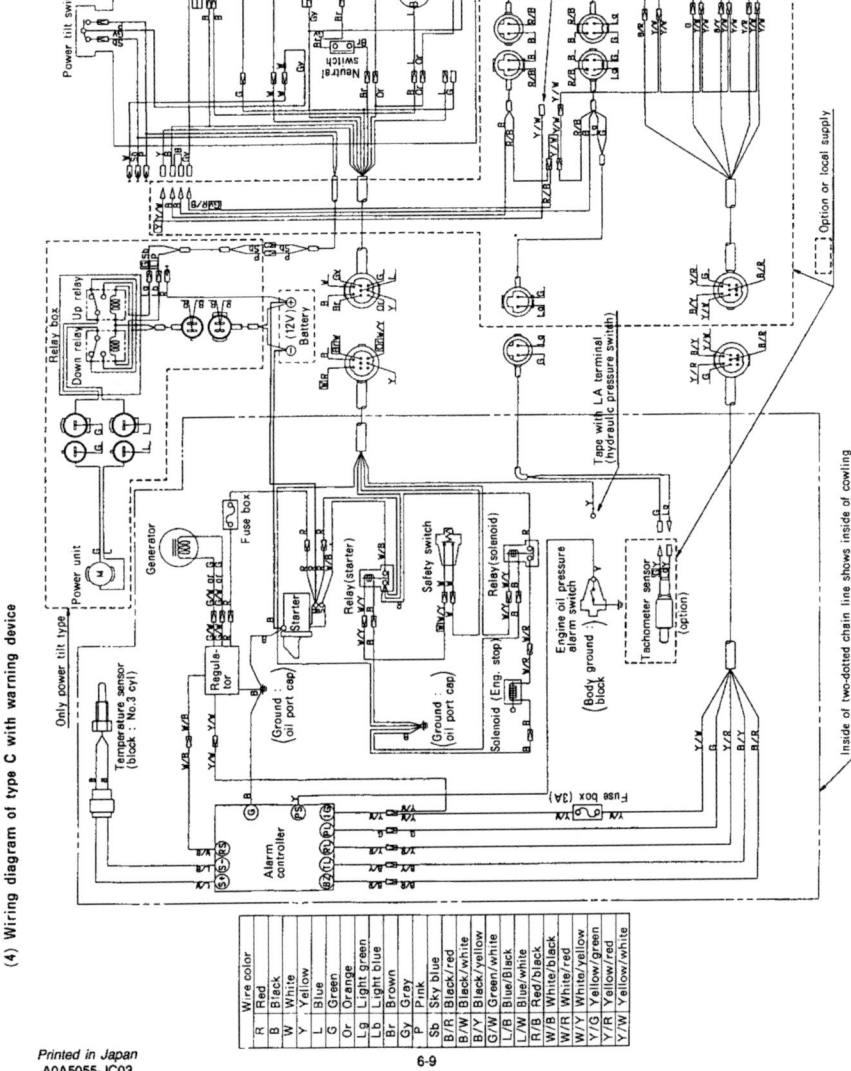

(4) Wiring diagram of type C with warning device

Chapter 6 Electric Equipment
4. Wiring Diagram

_SM/D27A & D36A_

(5) Wiring diagram of type D with warning device

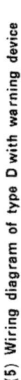

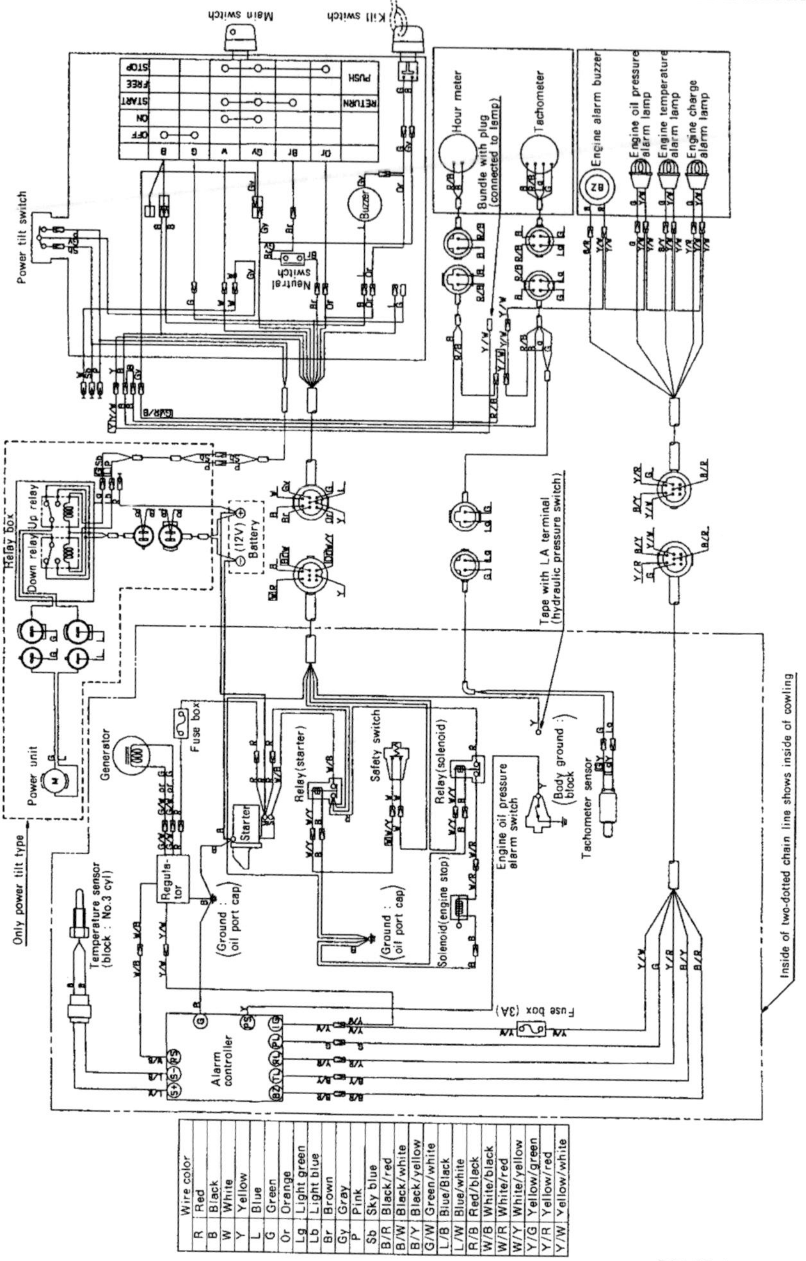

Wire color	
R	Red
B	Black
W	White
Y	Yellow
L	Blue
G	Green
Or	Orange
Lg	Light green
Lb	Light blue
Br	Brown
Gy	Gray
P	Pink
Sb	Sky blue
B/R	Black/red
B/W	Black/white
B/Y	Black/yellow
G/W	Green/white
L/B	Blue/black
L/W	Blue/white
R/B	Red/black
W/B	White/black
W/R	White/red
W/Y	White/yellow
Y/G	Yellow/green
Y/R	Yellow/red
Y/W	Yellow/white

Printed in Japan
A0A5055-JC03

CHAPTER 7
SERVICE STANDARD

1. Service Standard Table (Engine) 7-1
2. Service Standard Table (Drive Unit) 7-3

Chapter 7 Service Standard
1. Service Standard Table (Engine)

SM/D27A & D36A

1. Service Standard Table (Engine)

(1) D27A

(Unit : mm)

Item			Standard dimensions		Standard clearance during reassembling	Max. allowable clearance	Wear limit	Remarks
			Nominal dimensions	Dimensional tolerance				
Cylinder liner	Cylinder liner inside diameter	L	φ70	+0.030 +0.020	—	—	70.10	Reboring, if it exceeds the limit (Over size of 0.25)
		M	φ70	+0.020 +0.010				
		S	φ70	+0.010 0				
	Cylinder inside diameter roundness		—	—	—	—	—	—
Piston/piston pin	Piston outside diameter	L	φ69.940	+0.015 +0.005	—	—	69.88	
		M	φ69.940	±0.005				
		S	φ69.940	−0.005 −0.015				
	Clearance between piston outside dia. and cylinder liner inside dia.	L	—	—	—	0.13	—	
		M						
		S						
	Piston pin boss hole diameter		φ20	+0.008 0	0~0.017	0.1	—	
	Piston pin outside diameter			0 −0.009			19.90	
Piston ring/oil ring	Clearance between piston ring and ring groove	No.1 piston ring width		1.5	−0.010 −0.025	0.050~0.080	0.12	—
		No.1 piston ring groove width			+0.055 +0.040			
		No.2 piston ring width		1.5	−0.010 −0.025	0.030~0.060	0.12	—
		No.2 piston ring groove width			+0.035 +0.020			
		Oil ring width		3.5	−0.010 −0.025	0.020~0.050	0.12	—
		Oil ring groove width			+0.025 +0.010			
	End gap	No.1 and No.2 piston ring		—	—	0.20~0.35	1.2	—
		Oil ring				0.15~0.35		
Connecting rod	Crank pin outside diameter		φ36	0 −0.015	0.020~0.057	0.15	35.90	
	Crank pin metal inside diameter			+0.042 +0.020			36.08	
	Piston pin outside diameter		φ20	0 −0.009	0.025~0.047	0.1	19.90	
	Piston pin metal inside diameter			+0.038 +0.025			20.10	
	Parallelism between large end hole and small end hole		—	—	0.05/100mm	0.07/100mm	—	
Crankshaft	Crank journal outside diameter		φ40	0 −0.015	0.010~0.053	0.15	39.90	
	Crank main bearing inside diameter			+0.038 +0.010			40.08	
	Crankshaft side gap		—	—	0.15~0.45	0.6	—	
	Deflection (crank arm opening angle)		—	—				
	Center deviation		—	<0.03	—	0.05	—	
Cylinder head	Intake valve sinking		0.25	±0.1	—	0.5	—	
	Exhaust valve sinking		−0.50	±0.1	—	−0.25	—	
	Intake/exhaust valve, seat valve	Intake	(Tightening margin) 31.5	0.058~0.094		—	—	
		Exhaust	(Tightening margin) 26.5	0.050~0.083				

Printed in Japan
A0A5055-JC03

7-1

Chapter 7 Service Standard
1. Service Standard Table (Engine)

SM/D27A & D36A

(Unit : mm)

	Item			Standard dimensions		Standard clearance during reassembling	Max. allowable clearance	Wear limit	Remarks
				Nominal dimensions	Dimensional tolerance				
Intake/exhaust valve	Intake valve	Stem diameter		φ7	−0.030 −0.045	0.035~0.065	0.12	6.92	
		Valve guide inside diameter			+0.02 +0.005			7.08	
	Exhaust valve	Stem diameter		φ7	−0.03 −0.045	0.035~0.065	0.12	6.92	
		Valve guide inside diameter			+0.02 +0.005			7.08	
	Valve head thickness		Intake	—	—	—		0.20	0.3
			Exhaust						
Camshaft	Camshaft outside diameter			φ41	−0.050 −0.075	0.05~0.100	0.15	40.90	
	Camshaft bearing inside diameter				+0.025 0			41.07	
	Cam height		Intake	34.965	±0.03			34.87	
			Exhaust	34.965	±0.03	—	—	34.87	
			Fuel	33.436	±0.03			33.34	
Moving valve device	Intake/exhaust valve spring	Compressive force (at 1 mm compression)		2.37 1.87kgf				—	
		Free length		37.4	—	—	—	36	
		Inclination		1.6				2.0	
	Intake/exhaust valve arm shaft outside diameter			φ16	−0.016 −0.034	0.016~0.052	0.13	15.90	
	Intake/exhaust valve arm inside diameter				+0.018 0			16.03	
	Fuel valve arm shaft outside diameter			φ16	−0.016 −0.034	0.016~0.052	0.15	15.90	
	Fuel valve arm inside diameter				+0.018 0			16.03	

Chapter 7 Service Standard
1. Service Standard Table (Engine)

SM/D27A & D36A

(2) D36A

(Unit : mm)

	Item			Standard dimensions		Standard clearance during reassembling	Max. allowable clearance	Wear limit	Remarks
				Nominal dimensions	Dimensional tolerance				
Cylinder liner	Cylinder liner inside diameter		L	φ82	+0.030 / +0.020	—	—	82.10	Reboring, if it exceeds the limit. (Oversize of 0.25)
			M	φ82	+0.020 / +0.010				
			S	φ82	+0.010 / 0				
	Cylinder inside diameter roundness			0.01	—	—	—	0.03	
Piston/piston pin	Piston outside diameter		L	φ81.950	+0.015 / +0.005	—	—	81.88	
			M	φ81.950	±0.005				
			S	φ81.950	−0.005 / −0.015				
	Clearance between piston outside dia. and cylinder liner inside dia.		L	—	—	—	0.13	—	
			M						
			S						
	Piston pin boss hole diameter			φ26	+0.009 / 0	0~0.022	0.1	—	
	Piston pin outside diameter				0 / −0.013			25.90	
Piston ring/oil ring	Clearance between piston ring and ring groove	№1 piston ring width		2.0	−0.010 / −0.025	0.050~0.080	0.12	—	
		№1 piston ring groove width			+0.055 / +0.040				
		№2 piston ring width		2.0	−0.010 / −0.025	0.030~0.060	0.12	—	
		№2 piston ring groove width			+0.035 / +0.020				
		Oil ring width		3.5	−0.010 / −0.025	0.020~0.050	0.12	—	
		Oil ring groove width			+0.025 / +0.010				
	End gap	№1 and №2 piston ring		—	—	0.25~0.40	1.2	—	
		Oil ring				0.15~0.35			
Connecting rod	Crank pin outside diameter			φ44	0 / −0.015	0.024~0.061	0.15	43.90	
	Crank pin metal inside diameter				+0.046 / +0.024			44.08	
	Piston pin outside diameter			φ26	0 / −0.013	0.025~0.051	0.1	25.90	
	Piston pin metal inside diameter				+0.038 / +0.025			26.10	
	Parallelism between large end hole and small end hole			—	—	0.05/100mm	0.07/100mm	—	
Crankshaft	Crank journal outside diameter			φ50	0 / −0.015	0.010~0.056	0.15	49.9	
	Crank main bearing inside diameter				+0.041 / +0.010			50.08	
	Crankshaft side gap			—	—	0.15~0.45	0.6	—	
	Deflection (crank arm opening angle)			—	—	—	—	—	
	Center deviation			—	<0.03	—	0.05	—	
Cylinder head	Intake valve sinking			0.25	±0.1	—	0.5	—	
	Exhaust valve sinking			0.45	±0.1	—	0.7	—	
	Intake/exhaust valve, seat valve	Intake		(Tightening margin) 38		0.088~0.124	0.5	—	
		Exhaust		(Tightening margin) 33		0.067~0.103			

Chapter 7 Service Standard
1. Service Standard Table (Engine)

SM/D27A & D36A

(Unit : mm)

	Item			Standard dimensions		Standard clearance during reassembling	Max. allowable clearance	Wear limit	Remarks
				Nominal dimensions	Dimensional tolerance				
Intake/exhaust valve	Intake valve	Stem diameter		φ7	−0.030 −0.045	0.035~0.065	0.12	6.92	
		Valve guide inside diameter			+0.02 +0.005			7.08	
	Exhaust valve	Stem diameter		φ7	−0.03 −0.045	0.035~0.065	0.12	6.92	
		Valve guide inside diameter			+0.02 +0.005			7.08	
	Valve head thickness		Intake	—	—	—	0.20	0.3	
			Exhaust						
Camshaft	Camshaft outside diameter			φ49	−0.050 −0.075	0.05~0.100	0.15	48.90	
	Camshaft bearing inside diameter				+0.025 0			49.07	
	Cam height		Intake	41.928	±0.03			41.83	
			Exhaust	41.928	±0.03	—	—	41.83	
			Fuel	42.943	±0.03			42.84	
Moving valve device	Intake/exhaust valve spring	Compressive force (at 1 mm compression)		2.37 1.87kgf				—	
		Free length Outer/Inner		42.0/39.2 43.0/40.7	—	—	—	41.5/39.0	
		Inclination		1.6				2.0	
	Intake/exhaust valve arm shaft outside diameter			φ16	−0.016 −0.034	0.004~0.040	0.13	15.90	
	Intake/exhaust valve arm inside diameter				+0.006 −0.012			16.03	
	Fuel valve arm shaft outside diameter			φ22	−0.020 −0.041	0.005~0.047	0.15	21.88	
	Fuel valve arm inside diameter				+0.006 −0.015			22.03	

Chapter 7 Service Standard
2. Service Standard Table (Drive Unit)

SM/D27A & D36A

2. Service Standard Table (Drive Unit)

(1) D27A

(Unit : mm)

No.	Item	Standard dimensions		Standard clearance during reassembling	Max. allowable clearance
		Nominal dimensions	Dimensional tolerance		
1	Backlash between pinion and forward gear	—	—	0.1~0.25	0.8
2	Backlash between pinion and reverse gear	—	—	0.1~0.4	0.8
3	Forward gear bush inside diameter	φ20	+0.021 / 0	0.040~0.082	0.15
	Propeller shaft diameter		−0.040 / −0.061		
4	Cooling water pump key thickness	2.5	+0.008 / +0.002	—	Size 1.5
5	Cooling water pump outer plate thickness	1	—	—	Size 0.5
6	Cooling water pump impeller width	18.7	+0.1 / −0.2	0~0.5	0.65
	Cooling water pump insert	19	0 / −0.2		
	Swivel bracket hole diameter	φ36	+0.1 / 0		
7	Pivot shaft diameter	φ30	±0.3	0~1.1	—
	Bush wall thickness	3	−0.15 / −0.35		
8	Tilt lock lever shaft diameter	φ10	+0.020 / −0.058	0.06~0.174	0.4
	Sleeve bearing hole diameter		+0.116 / +0.080		
9	Bracket (shift) hole diameter	φ14	+0.05 / 0	0.1~0.393	0.6
	Bush wall thickness	0.9	±0.05		
	Shift shaft diameter	φ12	0 / −0.043		
10	Propeller shaft thrust clearance	—	—	0.3~0.5	0.6
11	Detent (shift) hole diameter	φ5	+0.15 / +0.05	0.05~0.198	0.4
	Pin (shift rod) shaft diameter		0 / −0.048		
	Shift rod hole diameter	φ5.1	±0.1	0~0.248	

Chapter 7 Service Standard
2. Service Standard Table (Drive Unit)

SM/D27A & D36A

(2) D36A

(Unit : mm)

No.	Item	Standard dimensions		Standard clearance during reassembling	Max. allowable clearance
		Nominal dimensions	Dimensional tolerance		
1	Backlash between pinion and forward gear	—	—	0.1~0.25	0.8
2	Backlash between pinion and reverse gear	—	—	0.1~0.4	0.8
3	Forward gear bush inside diameter	φ20	+0.021 / 0	0.040~0.082	0.15
	Propeller shaft diameter		−0.040 / −0.061		
4	Cooling water pump key thickness	4	+0.012 / +0.004	—	Size 2
5	Cooling water pump outer plate thickness	1	—	—	Size 0.5
6	Cooling water pump impeller width	25.75	±0.15	0~0.5	0.65
	Cooling water pump insert	26	±0.1		
7	Swivel bracket hole diameter	φ36	+0.1 / 0	0~1.1	—
	Pivot shaft diameter	φ30	±0.3		
	Bush wall thickness	3	−0.15 / −0.35		
8	Tilt lock lever shaft diameter	φ10	+0.020 / −0.058	0.06~0.174	0.4
	Sleeve bearing hole diameter		+0.116 / +0.080		
9	Bracket (shift) hole diameter	φ14	+0.05 / 0	0.1~0.393	0.6
	Bush wall thickness	0.9	±0.05		
	Shift shaft diameter	φ12	0 / −0.043		
10	Propeller shaft thrust clearance	—	—	0.3~0.5	0.6
11	Detent (shift) hole diameter	φ5	+0.15 / +0.05	0.05~0.198	0.4
	Pin (shift rod) shaft diameter		0 / −0.048		
	Shift rod hole diameter	φ5.1	±0.1	0~0.248	

CHAPTER 8
MAIN BOLT TIGHTENING TORQUE

1. Main Bolt Tightening Torque 8-1

Chapter 8 Main Bolt Tightening Torque
1. Main Bolt Tightening Torque   SM/D27A & D36A

1. Main Bolt Tightening Torque

1-1 Engine

○ encircled numbers show that engine parts differs for D27A and D36A.

No.	Tightened part	Screw size	Width	kgf-m Tightening torque	Remarks
①	Rod bolt	M 7×1.0 M 9×1.0	12 13	2.2~2.5 4.5~5.0	
②	Metal cap bolt	M10×1.5 M12×1.75	14 17	4.6~5.0 7.5~8.5	
3	Main bearing case auxiliary bolt	M 8×1.25	12	2.5~2.7	
④	Flywheel tightening nut	M16×1.5 M24×1.5	22 36	16.5~17.5 27.0~29.0	
⑤	Crank pulley tightening nut (crown nut)	M35×1.5 M42×2.0	–	16.5~17.5 17.5~18.5	
6	Hydraulic pressure switch	PT 1/8	24	2.5~3.0	
7	Injector tap set bolt	M 8×1.25	Hexagon rod 6	2.6~2.8	Hexagon hole bolt
8	Adjuster set bolt	M 4×0.7	Hexagon rod 3	0.08~0.11	Hexagon hole bolt
9	Cam pulley set bolt	M10×1.5	14	4.5~5.0	
10	Valve arm case set bolt	M 6×1.0	10	0.8~1.0	
11	Valve arm case set bolt	M 8×1.25	12	2.5~2.7	

Upper column for D27A

1-2 Drive Unit

No.	Tightened part	Screw size	Width	kgf-m Tightening torque	Remarks
1	Pinion gear tightening nut	M12×1.25	19	9.0~10.0	
2	Tilt tube tightening nut	UNF7/8	32	2.0	
3	Propeller nut (SUS)	M16×1.5	30	3.0~4.0	
4	Bearing housing tightening nut	M10	14	3.7~3.9	
5	Lower tightening bolt	M10	10	3.7~3.9	
6	CW pump case tightening bolt	M6	10	0.7~0.9	
7	Cylinder support set nut	M16×1.5	24	11.0~15.0	
8	Engine set bolt	M8	12	2.7~2.9	

Chapter 8 Main Bolt Tightening Torque
1. Main Bolt Tightening Torque

SM/D27A & D36A

1-3 Tightening torque of bolt and nut other than described on p. 8-1

Size	Tightening torque		Width
	7T bolt and nut	Stainless bolt and nut	
M 6	0.8~1.0kgf-m	0.7~0.9kgf-m	10
M 8	2.5~2.7kgf-m	1.9~2.1kgf-m	12
M10	4.5~5.0kgf-m	3.7~3.9kgf-m	14

NOTE:
1. Before tightening the bolts and nuts of the engine, apply lube oil to the screws and washers.
2. Before tightening the bolts and nuts of the lower unit, apply THREE BOND #1215 to the screws.
3. Before installing the propeller, apply grease (COSMO GREASE DYNAMAX EP No.2 or the equivalent) to the front surface of the propeller shaft spline.
4. When reassembling the mount rubber, be careful that no lube oil is on it.
5. Apply grease to the 3 greasing points (grease nipple MT6 X 1)until the grease overflows from both ends. (The grease must be COSMO GREASE DYNAMAX EP No.2 or the equivalent).
6. Bulge the pipe end, which is inserted into the rubber hose, as described on the diagram. Be sure to attach 2 hose clips on each side.

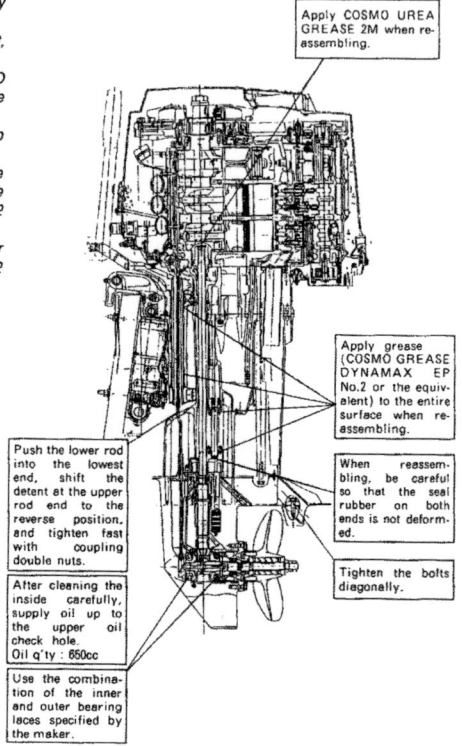

Apply COSMO UREA GREASE 2M when reassembling.

Apply grease (COSMO GREASE DYNAMAX EP No.2 or the equivalent) to the entire surface when reassembling.

When reassembling, be careful so that the seal rubber on both ends is not deformed.

Tighten the bolts diagonally.

Push the lower rod into the lowest end, shift the detent at the upper rod end to the reverse position, and tighten fast with coupling double nuts.

After cleaning the inside carefully, supply oil up to the upper oil check hole.
Oil q'ty : 650cc

Use the combination of the inner and outer bearing laces specified by the maker.

CHAPTER 9
BACKLASH ADJUSTMENT

1. Backlash Adjustment 9-1

Chapter 9 Backlash Adjustment
1. Backlash Adjustment

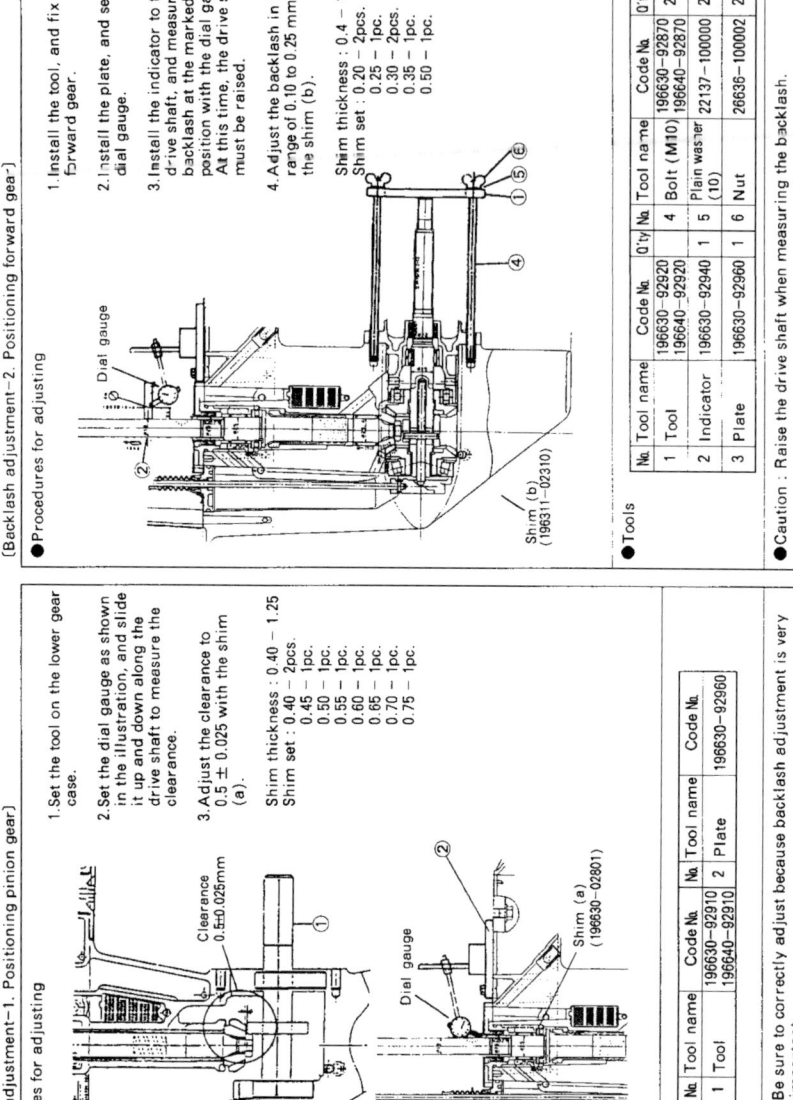

[Backlash adjustment-2. Positioning forward gear]

● Procedures for adjusting

1. Install the tool, and fix the forward gear.
2. Install the plate, and set the dial gauge.
3. Install the indicator to the drive shaft, and measure the backlash at the marked position with the dial gauge. At this time, the drive shaft must be raised.
4. Adjust the backlash in the range of 0.10 to 0.25 mm with the shim (b).

Shim thickness : 0.4 – 1.1
Shim set : 0.20 – 2pcs.
 0.25 – 1pc.
 0.30 – 2pcs.
 0.35 – 1pc.
 0.50 – 1pc.

Shim (b) (196311-02310)

● Tools

No.	Tool name	Code No.	Q'ty	No.	Tool name	Code No.	Q'ty
1	Tool	196630-92920 / 196640-92920		4	Bolt (M10)	196630-92870 / 196640-92870	2
2	Indicator	196630-92940	1	5	Plain washer (10)	22137-100000	2
3	Plate	196630-92960	1	6	Nut	26636-100002	2

● Caution : Raise the drive shaft when measuring the backlash.

[Backlash adjustment-1. Positioning pinion gear]

● Procedures for adjusting

1. Set the tool on the lower gear case.
2. Set the dial gauge as shown in the illustration, and slide it up and down along the drive shaft to measure the clearance.
3. Adjust the clearance to 0.5 ± 0.025 with the shim (a).

Shim thickness : 0.40 – 1.25
Shim set : 0.40 – 2pcs.
 0.45 – 1pc.
 0.50 – 1pc.
 0.55 – 1pc.
 0.60 – 1pc.
 0.65 – 1pc.
 0.70 – 1pc.
 0.75 – 1pc.

Clearance 0.5±0.025mm

Shim (a) (196630-02801)

● Tools

No.	Tool name	Code No.	No.	Tool name	Code No.
1	Tool	196630-92910 / 196640-92910	2	Plate	196630-92960

● Caution : Be sure to correctly adjust because backlash adjustment is very important.

Chapter 9 Backlash Adjustment
1. Backlash Adjustment

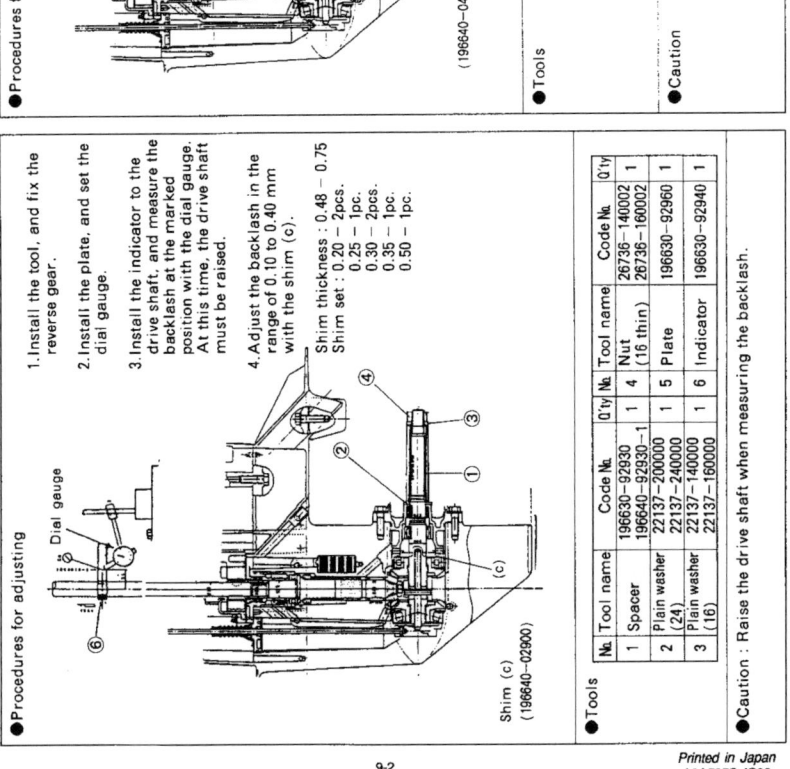

[Backlash adjustment–4. Positioning propeller shaft]

● Procedures for adjusting

1. Set the dial gauge at the tip of propeller shaft, and measure the thrust clearance.
2. Adjust the thrust clearance in the range of 0.3 to 0.5 mm with the collar (d).

   Collar set :
   2.6
   2.8
   3.0

(196640-04260)

● Tools

● Caution

[Backlash adjustment–3. Positioning reverse gear]

● Procedures for adjusting

1. Install the tool, and fix the reverse gear.
2. Install the plate, and set the dial gauge.
3. Install the indicator to the drive shaft, and measure the backlash at the marked position with the dial gauge. At this time, the drive shaft must be raised.
4. Adjust the backlash in the range of 0.10 to 0.40 mm with the shim (c).

Shim thickness : 0.48 – 0.75
Shim set : 0.20 – 2pcs.
           0.25 – 1pc.
           0.30 – 2pcs.
           0.35 – 1pc.
           0.50 – 1pc.

Shim (c)
(196640-02900)

● Tools

No.	Tool name	Code No.	Q'ty	No.	Tool name	Code No.	Q'ty
1	Spacer	196630-92930	1	4	Nut (16 thin)	26736-140002	1
		196640-92930	1			26736-160002	1
2	Plain washer (24)	22137-200000	1	5	Plate	196630-92960	1
		22137-240000	1				
3	Plain washer (16)	22137-140000	1	6	Indicator	196630-92940	1
		22137-160000	1				

● Caution : Raise the drive shaft when measuring the backlash.

CHAPTER 10
PERIODICAL INSPECTION

1. Periodical Inspection Table 10-1

Chapter 10 Periodical Inspection
1. Periodical Inspection Table _____SM/D27A & D36A

1. Periodical Inspection Table

● : Performed by YANMAR agency
○ : Inspected by user
◎ : Replaced parts by user

Item	Inspection	Inspection interval				
		Daily	Every 50 hours (or 1 month)	Every 100 hours (or 3 months)	Every 200 hours (or 6 months)	Every 400 hours (or 1 year)
Fuel	Check the tank oil level, or refuel	○				
	Clean the tank			○		
	Replace the filter					◎
Lube oil	Check, refuel or replace the engine lube oil	○	○ (Replace for the first time)	◎ (Replace)		
	Replace the lower unit lube oil		◎ (10 hours later at the beginning)	◎ (Replace)		
	Replace the filter element		◎ (First time)			◎
Cooling water (sea water side)	Check the discharge of cooling water	○				
	Replace the anti-corrosive zinc					◎
	Check (replace) the impeller					●
	Check the thermostat					●
Cylinder head	Adjust the intake/exhaust valve head clearance					●
Check/adjust the unit injector						●
Check/adjust the cable						●
Check the timing belt						●
Tighten the through bolt more securely			○			
Electrical equipment	Check the warning devices	○				
	Check the battery liquid level		○			
Apply grease					○	●
Replace the timing belt		1200Hr				

Others:

(1) When the unit is not used for more than 2 or 3 days:

- Land the ship, or tilt up the unit.
- Put a cover over the outboard motor.
- Remove the battery cable.

(2) Inspect or service the unit once a year or every 400 hours.

CHAPTER 11
OPTION

1. Diesel Outboard Propeller Guard Holes 11-1

1. Diesel Outboard Propeller Guard Holes

We have been requested to add the above option for our Diesel Outboard.

We have settled an option of "Propeller Guard Holes" which enable to fit a local made propeller guard securely without worrying about possible corrosion at holes.

1-1 Propeller Guard Hole (Lower Case)

Applicable model : D27X(Y)E
　　　　　　　　　　D36XAE
　　　　　　　　　　D36YE

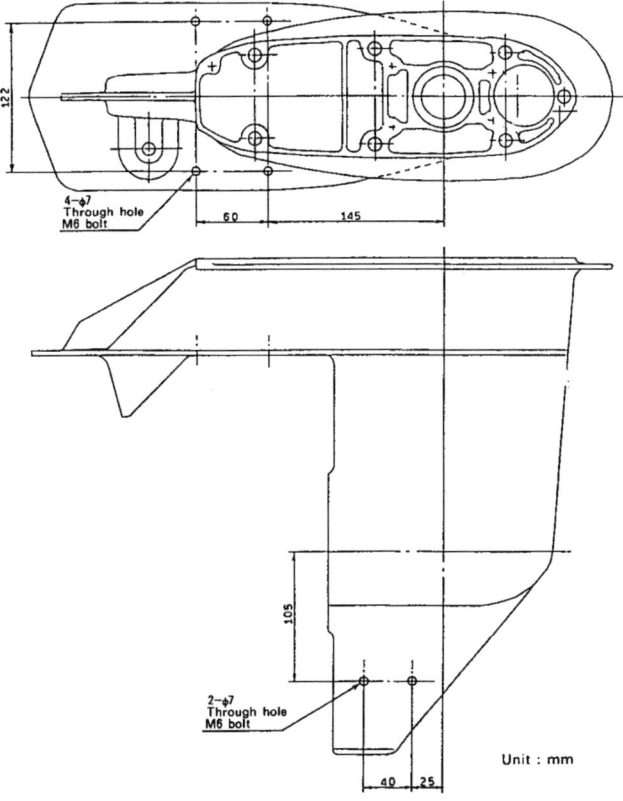

Unit : mm